HOMES
for creative living

Jeremy Jones

D1602167

CHRONICLE BOOKS • **SAN FRANCISCO**

Printed in the United States of America.

Library of Congress Cataloging in Publication Data

Jones, Jeremy A.
   Homes for creative living.

   1. Architect-designed houses—Designs and plans.
I. Title.
NA7125.J6   1984   728.3′7′0222   84-15623
ISBN 0-87701-314-4

Illustrations: Jeremy Jones
Text editing and development: Pamela Simon
Book and cover design: Susan Ficca

Chronicle Books
870 Market Street
San Francisco, CA 94102

In recent years there has been an increased demand for home designs that would solve the dilemma of the high cost and future scarcity of energy. All too often homes have been designed with energy savings as the major goal, while the original purpose of the structure—to provide a home for people—was forgotten. A variety of strange forms have been presented as ultimate homes of the future. Although the designs are supported by elaborate graphs, heat-loss calculations, sun-angle diagrams, and extensive studies, we are left wondering who the people are who will occupy these homes of the future. These homes seem to be designed for a standardized, trend-accepting young couple whose personality is a blend of several television-drama personalities. For most of us, a private way of life is very important. Both the larger patterns of our lives and the individual day-to-day ways in which we live should and can influence the design of our homes. It is possible to create a home design that reflects an individual lifestyle and still incorporates energy-saving methods to enhance the owner's enjoyment and comfort.

After designing several homes and seeing them through their first seasons, it was apparent to me that a wide variety of energy-saving techniques could be effective. By combining various methods of energy conservation, a wide array of home designs could be produced that would answer the needs of many different lifestyles, climates, and sites. The needs and personalities of my clients had made each home I designed unique in shape, plan, use of materials, and energy systems, and yet each house passed through the most severe seasons comfortably and economically. It was not necessary to carry any one energy-saving technique to extremes as long as several carefully integrated methods could act together. It had initially seemed to me like a compromise to make advances in the technology of earth sheltering, passive solar heating, insulation,

and other techniques secondary to the design wishes of the client. But I came to realize that the variety of family activities that each house supported justified a more complex approach to design.

Critics of earth-sheltered houses have claimed that "you can't sell anything you can't see." This claim was proven wrong when the first "underground" homes began to attract attention for their dramatic savings in power consumption and for their unique designs. Many of my first home-design commissions resulted from publicity following the construction of an earth home. It had been designed for a couple who had difficulty locating an architect willing to attempt a project in this still-experimental form of housing. Each new client had an interest in earth sheltering and other ways of saving energy and money, but each person also had a unique viewpoint and need. One wanted a totally buried house to avoid noises from a nearby airport, while another was primarily interested in taking advantage of a site that was difficult to build a conventional house on but had spectacular views. A farmer was interested in underground housing because he noticed that his rabbits were more comfortable than his family. The rabbits lived in an insulated and mounded structure while his family had a plywood ranch house.

As the first earth-sheltered homes reached the design stage it became time to sell the concept to building-code officials and bankers. On one occasion, a group of legislators stood patiently outside an underground home to hear a lecture on the house and to gather their courage to explore the interior. Accepting the unknown as part of their job, they moved bravely toward the door. Although the door was normal in size, each person stooped while entering the unusual house. Ready for a Neanderthal setting of scattered bones, cold rock, and sleeping bats, they found instead a brightly lit

tropical garden, a twenty-five-mile view, and a floor plan so open that it allowed a seventy-foot unobstructed interior view from corner to corner. Several walls stopped short of the ceiling to admit light from other areas. The house was simple enough that the owner, who had no building experience, had constructed most of it himself. From inside there was no way to tell that the home was underground. As one senator observed, "I guess you can't see through a stud wall either."

Subsequent clients came along who wanted to save energy, or at least money, but would not consider earth sheltering. This led to the development of employing greenhouses in the designs for the purpose of collecting solar heat, as well as the use of a variety of other systems, until there seemed to be a different system for each client's needs and lifestyle.

As more opportunities to design homes developed, it became clear to me that there was a greater challenge in designing homes appropriate to the needs of the client than in just employing currently popular energy-conservation techniques in the designs. The most vital and interesting homes are settings for the excitement of living, using scientific principles to support the initial design concept of a unique home for a unique family or individual. People are not mere consumers of BTU's and kilowatts who occupy cleverly engineered dwellings. Our homes should reflect our aspirations, values, and way of life. It is hoped that the ideas presented in the following pages will stimulate your thinking as you plan your special home.

Although no stock plans are available for the houses shown in this book, permission is granted for use of this material as a basis for the development of your own design. The illustrations and the text in this book are copyrighted, so written permission is required for republication in any form.

Contents

Designing for Personal Preference ___ 67

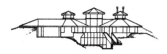

Designing Just for Fun ___ 91

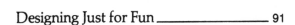

Designing for Living

The first time a person becomes involved in the design of his own home, it's very difficult to get past preconceptions. People often go to extremes in selecting a floor plan or style. When a design begins with an existing plan or an existing home, the house has been remodeled before it's off the

---

When a design begins with an existing plan or an existing home, the house has been remodeled before it's off the drawing board.

---

drawing board. More satisfying designs begin with a fundamental analysis of the current and future activities of the people who will live in the houses. For you, the future occupant of a custom-designed home, that means taking a look at how long you expect to live in the home and how your life will change during that time. The home is the setting for most of our activities and influences their effectiveness. Before any special design or style is selected, a plan must be developed that serves your individual needs.

Designing for Living

A young couple walked into an architect's office with a manila envelope stuffed with clippings of house plans collected from all the magazines they had read over the past year while standing in the grocery checkout line. Seeming quite confident, the husband said, "We have a pretty good idea of what we want in our house. Maybe a floor plan like this," and then he started digging through the stack. The wife, looking over his shoulder, added, "Well, not quite like that because I want a library—I used to love talking to my grandfather in the library when I was a little girl." Again the husband went for the file. "A plan more like this but with a hot tub off the master bedroom and . . ." "Actually we have a list," the wife interrupted as she searched her purse and found a long piece of paper. Just under a long list of groceries was "master bedroom with hot tub, library, patio, three bedrooms, family room, chopping block in kitchen, and doorbell that plays 'South Rampart Street Parade.'" The list and file consisted of a conglomeration of labeled rooms, but little thought had been given to the activities that would take place in the new home.

Planning a home starts with defining the personal values of the future occupants. Often it means making decisions not required when purchasing a pre-designed home. Rather than being a process that ends up in divorce, it can be a positive learning experience. It is an opportunity to make new beginnings and to reassess your values. It requires open minds seeking new possibilities.

Many people, like the couple in the example, arrive at the architect's office with what they think is a plan they want and with the hope that the architect will just "show us what it will look like." The wife wanted a library because she had happy memories of a similar room, but would a library really serve the needs of her present situation? Perhaps what she really needed was a computer room! A hot tub may be a good idea, but can the rest of the family use it if it's off the master bedroom? It may well be that each of these ideas would fit perfectly into the final plan, but a better plan would emerge from a study of family activities rather than special house features.

The first major issue to deal with in home design is that of time. How long will you live in this house? How old will you and your family be when you leave? What changes will time make in your present needs and preferences? Locked in the concerns of the moment, many couples have difficulty thinking how they will feel about the home they are planning just five years into the future. Answers to these questions will begin to set your priorities and lead to an appropriate and workable plan.

All the homes shown in this book started with a listing and grouping of family activities. These include not only the obvious everyday activities, but also hobbies, social activities, seasonal activities, and special events. They also include pastimes such as watching the fire, reading a book, or gazing at the view. The activities are then organized into groups that can share facilities and those that need to be separated. For instance, many people find that their sleeping area, rather than remaining unused all day, can also be a reading nook or a sewing area. As the functions of the spaces become more specific, each minor activity with its necessary equipment, furnishings, and lighting can be visualized until activity spaces begin to emerge.

Each activity area needs to be defined before a pattern for the entire house can be attempted. Each area is studied for compatibility with potential neighboring activities. Do these functions generate noise, odor, or distracting motion? Which utilities (plumbing and electrical) can be shared? Are activities that seem incompatible separated by the times of day when they are used? For example, a teenage girl can study in the same space used by a younger boy for practicing drums if they are not there at the same time.

The next step is to form connections or divisions between activity areas. Connections can be corridors, steps, or simply a lack of divisions. Division or separation can be achieved with a change of level, a piece of furniture, a screen, or a wall. The type and subtlety of each connection or separation shapes the character of your home.

Providing just enough area for each activity gives a space-capsule solution to design; everything can be reached when needed, every activity anticipated can be accommodated. For longer periods of habitation people need space and interesting nuances for their own sakes. The amount of space you will need and how it will be furnished is a very personal decision. For some people a large and simple space suggests tranquility and comfort. For others, such a space is boring and inhuman. They prefer smaller, more complex, cozy rooms. Still others need a variety of spatial experiences.

The following review of activity-oriented design issues can be used as a checklist in organizing spaces to develop a plan.

1. How long will you live in this house?
   a. Will you live here for the rest of your life? If not, how old will you and other family members be when you move again?
   b. Will there be more or fewer people living in the house in the future?
   c. Do you expect to build the entire house now or to add to it later?
   d. How will the landscaping and the other aspects of your site change?
   e. What development or other changes will take place near your property?

2. How will you get to your house?
   a. Is there more than one way to drive onto your site?
   b. What is the best way for pedestrians to reach your house?
   c. What do you most want to see as you approach the house?
   d. Do you need more than one way to get into the house? (For example: a mudroom, a pass-through door for shop or building materials, extra-large doors, etc.)

3. List all regular, special, and seasonal activities of those who will live in the house; include hobbies and passive activities.
   a. Group activities into those that could use the same space even if carried out at different times.

b. Examples of activity groupings:
   1. Living areas (could include several different areas): sitting, talking, reading, looking at a view, watching TV, talking on the phone, studying, working on business, operating a computer, planning trips, playing games, entertaining, listening to music, rehearsing, watching slides or movies, playing with toys, writing, etc.
   2. Craft areas: sewing, weaving, quilting, painting, drawing, glass work, woodwork and carving, pottery and ceramics, working with plants, etc.
   3. Eating areas: general cooking, salad making, canning, freezing, bread making, food storage, utensil and equipment storage, formal dining, snacking, drinking, entertaining, etc.
   4. Private areas: sleeping, intimate activities, convalescence, dressing, applying make-up, bathing, infant care, storage of clothes, storage of medicines, storage of linens, etc.
   5. Shops: carpentry, metal and plastic work, general repair, vehicle maintenance, bike shop, electronics shop, etc.
   6. Garage and general storage
   7. Special functions: greenhouse, hot tub, sauna, pool, sport court, gazebo, gardens, pet facilities, darkroom, etc.
   c. Determine which activities must be separated and in what way.
   d. Determine the most efficient arrangement of activity groups based on frequency of use and spatial connections and divisions.

4. List equipment and special furnishings for each activity.
   a. Determine the space (area and ceiling height) required for the most space-consuming activity in each division and the additional space required for equipment or furnishings for all activities in that category. For some activities, equipment will be stored elsewhere, so don't forget that storage areas for this equipment must be allowed for in your design.
   b. Schematically arrange the relative position of all furnishings within each area.

5. Adjust the activity diagrams to accommodate external influences such as view, sunlight, and noise.

6. Imagine a variety of activities taking place in your future home and see if the arrangements still work. Imagine activities taking place five, ten, and twenty years from now as the ages of residents change.

7. Now move on to the next chapters and consider the design influences of your house site, the historical influences of your area, and the things you might do with your house just for fun.

9

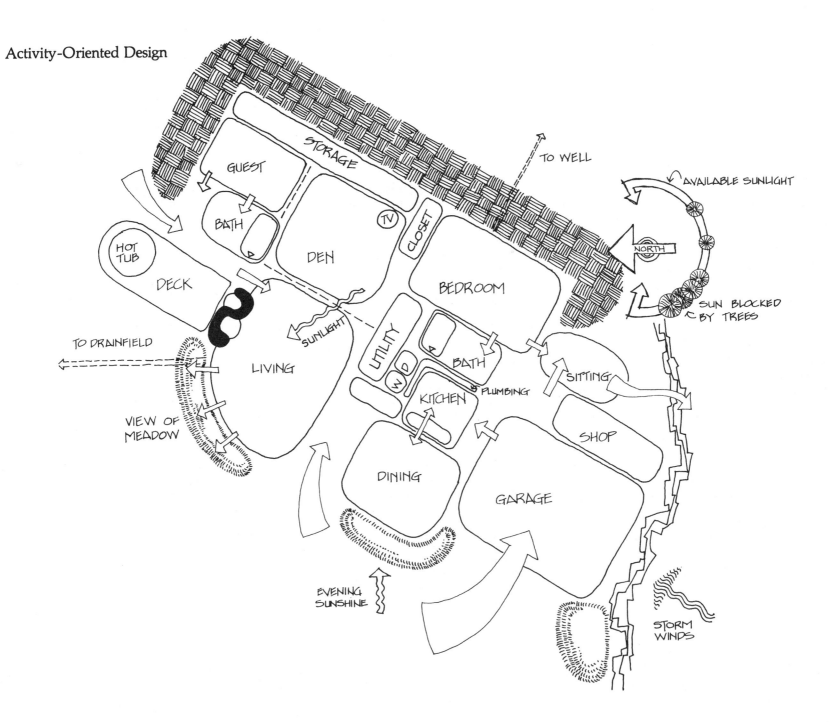

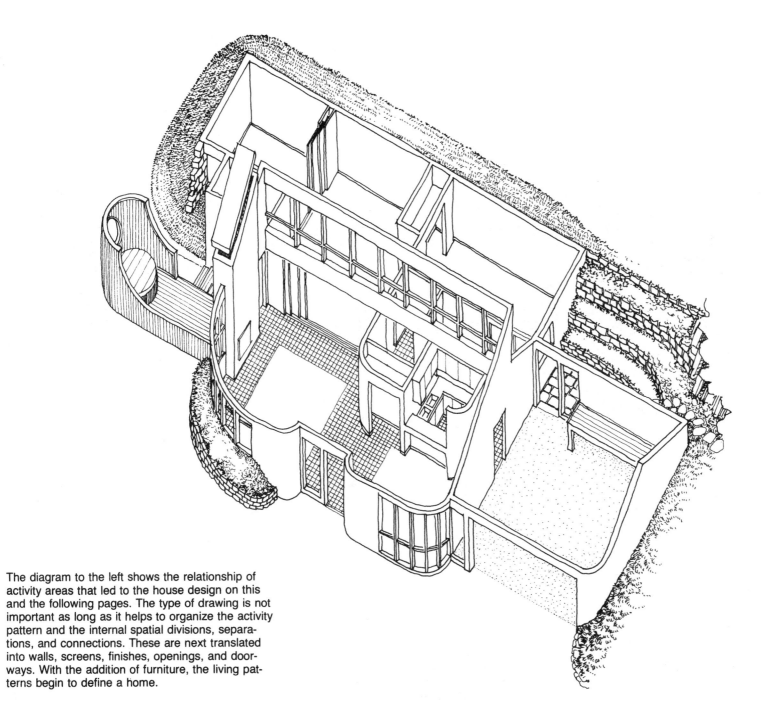

The diagram to the left shows the relationship of
activity areas that led to the house design on this
and the following pages. The type of drawing is not
important as long as it helps to organize the activity
pattern and the internal spatial divisions, separa-
tions, and connections. These are next translated
into walls, screens, finishes, openings, and door-
ways. With the addition of furniture, the living patterns begin to define a home.

Movable-Wall Home 1650 square feet

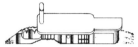

The site for this home seemed to present a variety of problems. Since the house was to be on the approach path to a major airport, the meadow view was to the north, and a continuous raised basalt outcropping bordered the south side, the usual methods of orientation for active and passive solar design would have been inadequate. The problems of the site had to be kept in mind as a functional design solution was developed.

The client wanted protection from weather and aircraft noise, but at the same time he wanted a light, open, and flexible living area. Eventually a concept emerged of a chain of spaces with furnishings or movable walls providing dividers. The living room is the main activity area, so it focuses out onto the

view, is the visual focus for other spaces, and receives direct sunlight from southeast-facing clerestory windows. The outside wall curves to provide both a panoramic view and greater continuity with adjacent spaces. The den can be separated from the living room by sliding panels, but the dining room is segmented only by furnishings and by the position of the main entry door. The kitchen is open above the counter so that it doesn't seem too detached.

The back half of the structure is underground for noise reduction and energy savings. The bedroom opens onto a small courtyard rimmed by the natural basalt wall. The guest area can be an extension of the den when the folding or sliding wall is open. Although this is not a large house, it can accommodate a very large gathering when required.

A secluded deck includes a hot tub and a barbecue for frequent entertaining. Trails near the deck lead to the meadow and woods.

The garage is large enough to include a bicycle-repair and construction area, with a view into the courtyard.

Curved edges on the walls, the hot tub enclosure, and the roof soften the external image of the home and give it a unique look without greatly increasing construction costs. The curved edges are most easily constructed by placing vertical siding over two thin plywood layers.

As a secondary benefit, the upper windows can be washed from outside by walking up the grass roof. From inside, the view through these windows is into the tops of windblown pines, Sunlight is controlled through all windows by multicolored miniblinds that reveal a graphic design when closed. The blinds are located between double panes of glass for greater insulation value and less dust accumulation. Suspended glass prisms near the high windows catch sunlight and refract it into changing colored patterns on the wall throughout the morning. Inside the house the mood is one of openness penetrated by natural light and yet it also conveys the feeling of a quiet and private retreat for the owner.

Although the design solution on the previous two pages was appropriate to the client, it was not the only way a house with this floor plan could have looked. Here are three other ways the house could have looked.

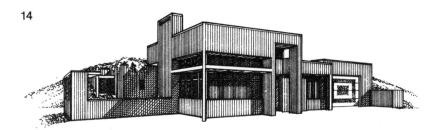

a. The first alternative is built in simple rectangular shapes with flat roofs. Every element of the home is designed with straight lines and a minimum of details. Visual interest is derived from changing shadows and use of materials.

b. The second house uses currently popular shapes and details to evoke historical forms and decorations. Such designs are not only interesting, they can be amusing. The external grid allows a subtle banding of color and an interesting progression of details. Although most forms are fairly simple, unusual details have been incorporated at entries and chimney tops.

c. The third alternative has sod on all of the roofs although there is still enough slope over the living room to allow for a clerestory window between roof levels. Everything is kept bold and simple to create an appearance of permanence.

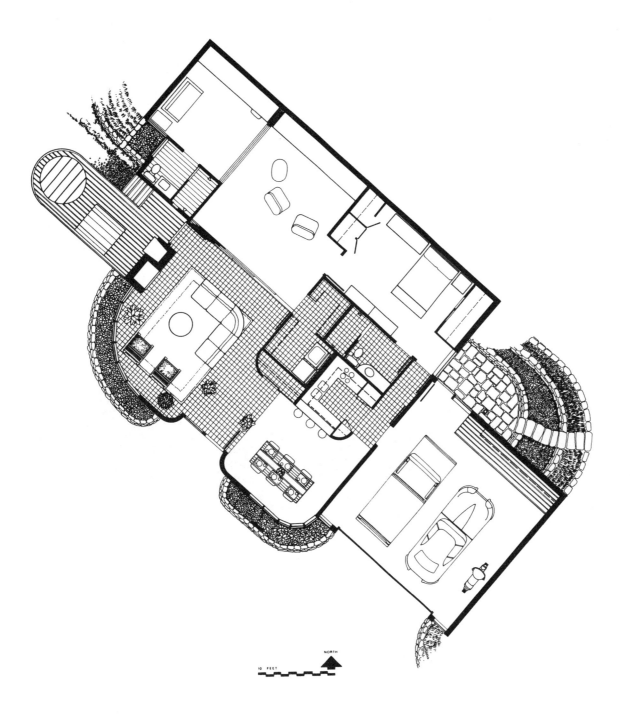

NORTH

10 FEET

Floating-Roof Home 1950 square feet

16 When earth sheltering was still something of a novelty, it was easy for architects to get defensive about designing "caves." Fortunately, several designers began to use a combination of an earth-mounded north side of a house for privacy and a passive-solar south side for daytime activities. The design shown here is similar to a house I designed to carry the "anti-cave" idea still further. The major structural supports for the south side of the house are pillars that are detached from the wall. Since they carry the roof load, the entire south wall can

take an irregular form as long as it's attached to the floor and the roof. Here the curve of the wall started as an attempt to harmonize with the piano in shape, but the idea of a freely flowing divider between inside and out became a main design feature. With only the ripple in the wall to divide three rooms in a row, it seemed that another form of emphasis might help. By varying the ceiling height in each room, a

series of spaces was created between the roofs. The spaces were filled with glass rather than a solid material so that daylight could shine directly or reflect into most of the south area of the house. With "no visible means of support," the roofs seem to float above the spaces in a very uncavelike manner. Although the back three sides of the house are mounded up to eight feet above floor level except at

the windows, there is no clue from inside that the house is earth-sheltered.

Most of the earth for mounding resulted from excavation, but more was added from nearby on the site. The dirt was pushed into position at the end of a hot August day so it was warm initially and didn't need to be heated by the house.

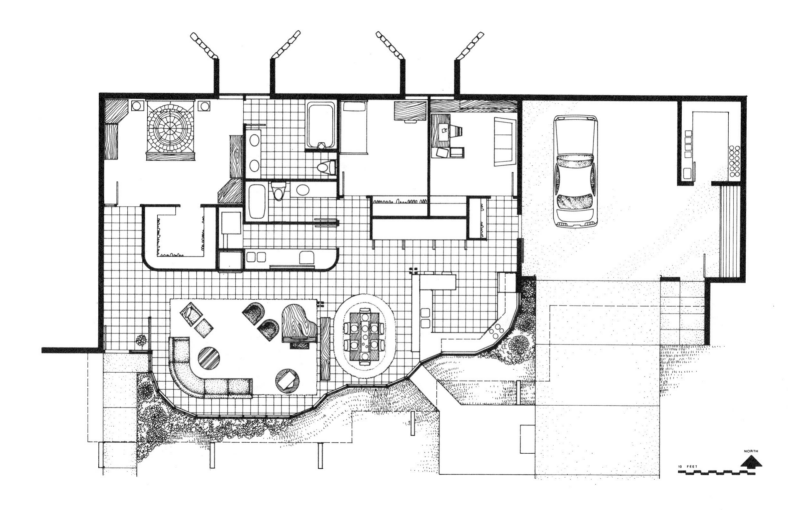

NORTH

10 FEET

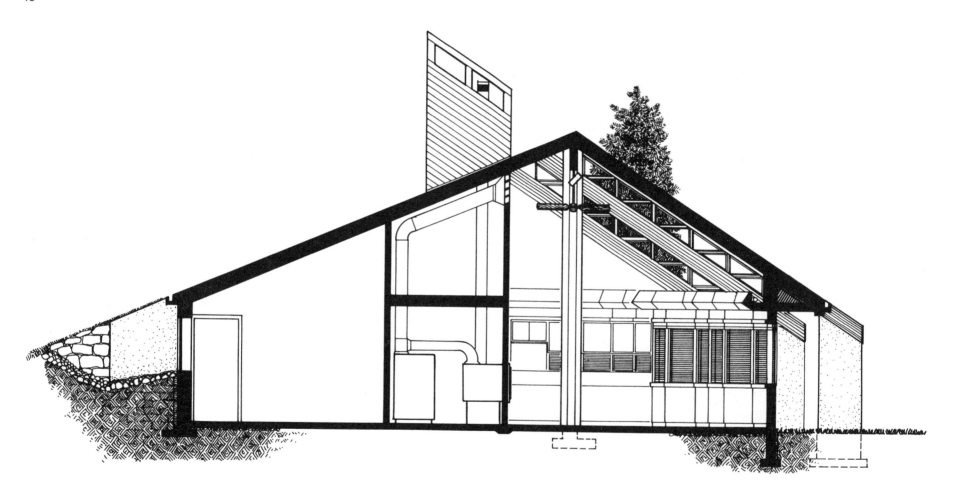

A metal roof was used for safety from grass fires, and metal covers were used for the tops of exposed beams.

At night, light from the interior spills onto the roofs as well as out of the front windows to give an almost tentlike lightness to this home when seen from outdoors.

Hexagonal Home 1600 square feet

20 Large homes with diverse functions and specialized rooms often require complex shapes. Small homes can be so simple that we enclose them with simple geometric shapes. In this plan two slightly related items, the chimney from the stove and the exhaust vent from the cooking hood, appear as identical features on the exterior of the house in order to maintain a simple appearance. The floor plan varies from overall symmetry only enough to allow for functional differences in the bedroom areas. The plan also groups plumbing fixtures into a relatively small area and makes the kitchen the focus of the home. A masonry wall for storing solar heat separates the kitchen from the living area. It has a pass-through opening to facilitate use of the stove for cooking (a portion of the heat emitted by the stove is also stored in the masonry wall).

Although the front room seems to be three distinct areas—dining room, entry, and sitting area—it was planned as one large sunlit space where furniture could be rearranged for different functions and occasions. Such informality accommodates the sort of living we experience in a vacation cabin. With the large glass area in the roof, a range of temperature would be experienced in the front rooms. The rooms in the back of the house are protected by insulation and earth mounding so they would have more stable temperatures.

Rainwater on the roof is diverted away from the glass area to open-faced drains down the two front corners of the wall.

The occupant's taste in color and fabric would be visible in the window blinds or curtains. Shades that are coiled at the base of the window and pulled up when needed would be the most effective window covering for this house—particularly for the non-rectangular roof windows.

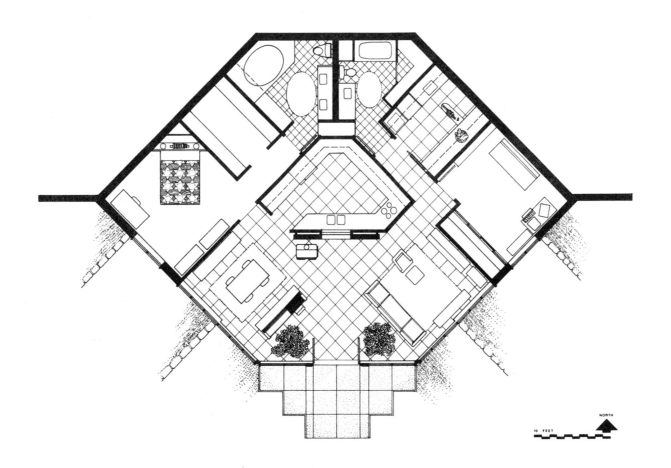

NORTH

10 FEET

Central-Greenhouse Home 2200 square feet

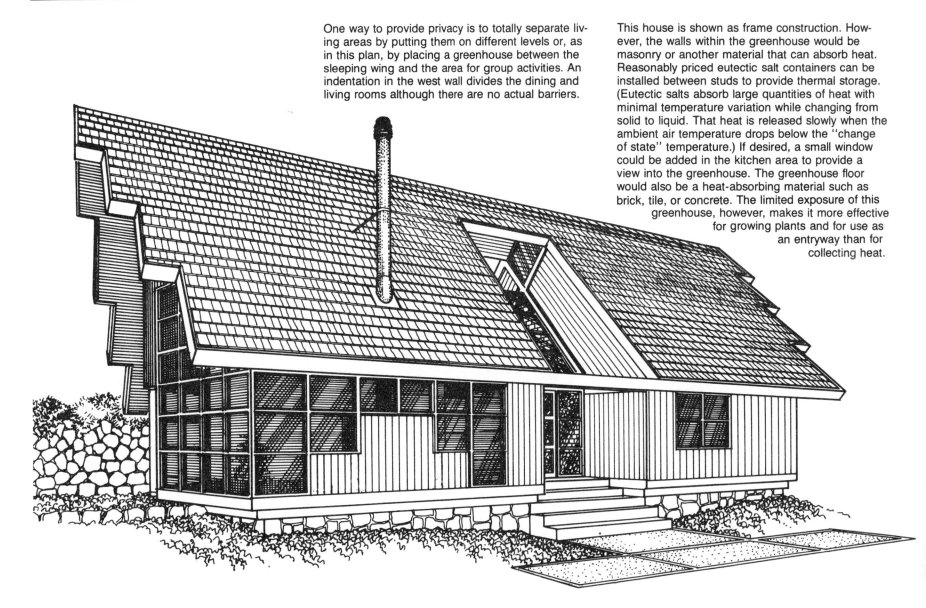

One way to provide privacy is to totally separate living areas by putting them on different levels or, as in this plan, by placing a greenhouse between the sleeping wing and the area for group activities. An indentation in the west wall divides the dining and living rooms although there are no actual barriers.

This house is shown as frame construction. However, the walls within the greenhouse would be masonry or another material that can absorb heat. Reasonably priced eutectic salt containers can be installed between studs to provide thermal storage. (Eutectic salts absorb large quantities of heat with minimal temperature variation while changing from solid to liquid. That heat is released slowly when the ambient air temperature drops below the "change of state" temperature.) If desired, a small window could be added in the kitchen area to provide a view into the greenhouse. The greenhouse floor would also be a heat-absorbing material such as brick, tile, or concrete. The limited exposure of this greenhouse, however, makes it more effective for growing plants and for use as an entryway than for collecting heat.

In the master bedroom the bath area is only slightly concealed from the rest of the room. This is for people who like to take long baths but do not like to be in a small room for a long time. The indented light wells in this room (and in the kitchen) are not required for emergency exiting, so they are just large enough to admit light and provide a nearby view of plants.

Notice that when a chimney is located on an exterior wall with a sloping roof, the chimney must be quite tall. By building code, the chimney must extend at least two feet higher than any part of the roof within ten feet. Local conditions may make this inadequate, particularly in areas over two thousand feet above sea level. Local building officials should be able to provide advice on this and many other local code restrictions and environmental influences.

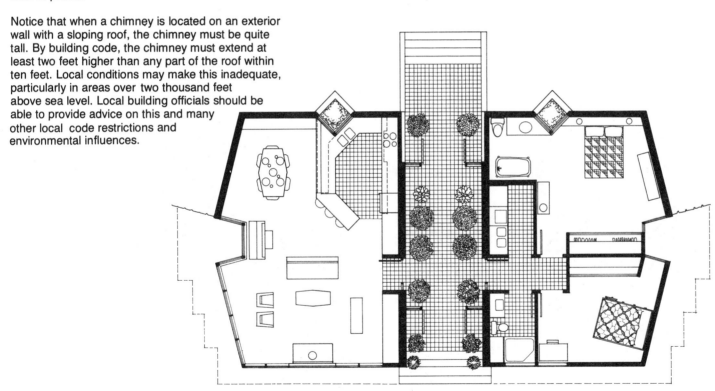

10 FEET

NORTH

Diagonal-Roof Home One 1940 square feet

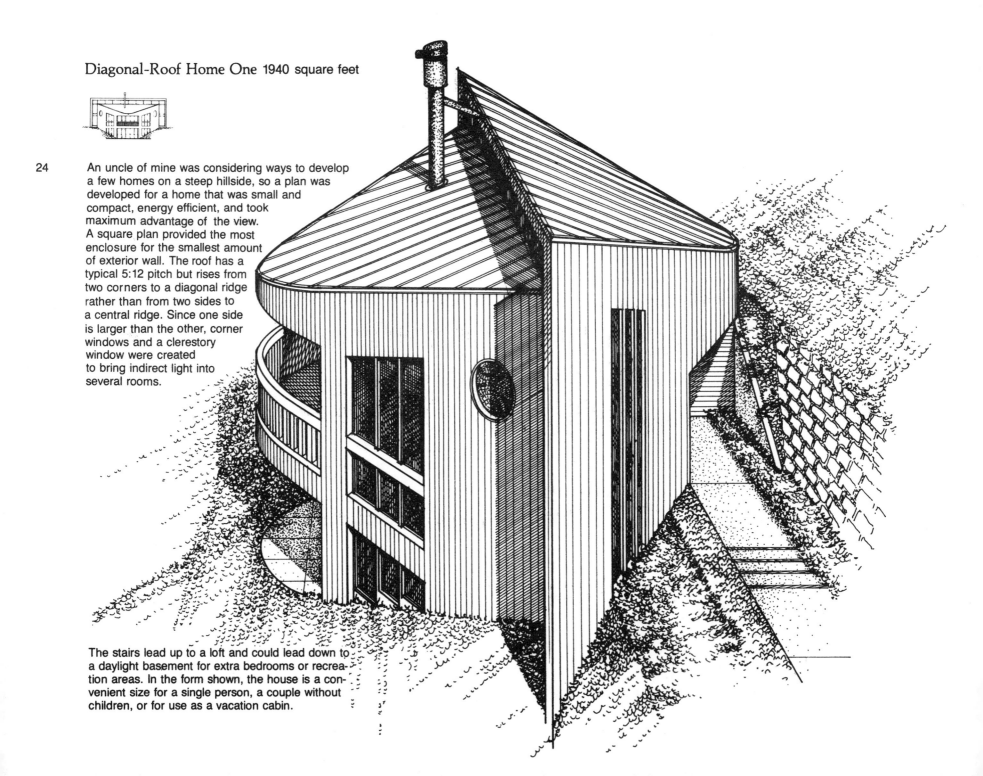

24　An uncle of mine was considering ways to develop
a few homes on a steep hillside, so a plan was
developed for a home that was small and
compact, energy efficient, and took
maximum advantage of the view.
A square plan provided the most
enclosure for the smallest amount
of exterior wall. The roof has a
typical 5:12 pitch but rises from
two corners to a diagonal ridge
rather than from two sides to
a central ridge. Since one side
is larger than the other, corner
windows and a clerestory
window were created
to bring indirect light into
several rooms.

The stairs lead up to a loft and could lead down to
a daylight basement for extra bedrooms or recreation areas. In the form shown, the house is a convenient size for a single person, a couple without
children, or for use as a vacation cabin.

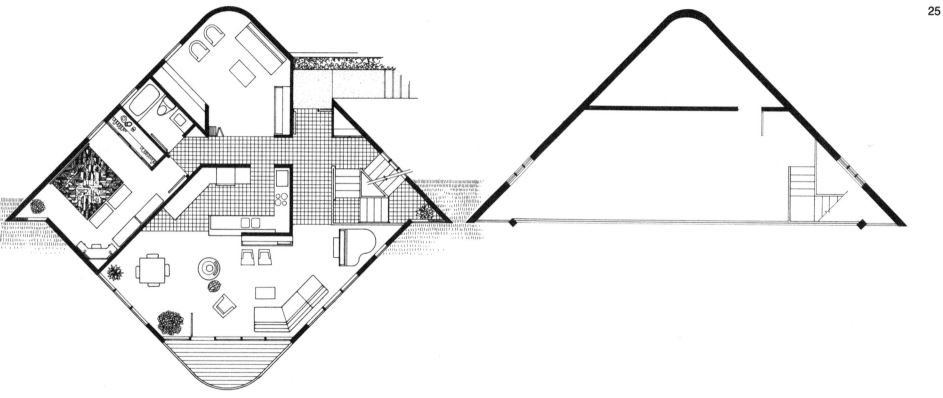

The plan places the kitchen centrally between the living room, the dining area, and a den that can be used as a guest room or bedroom. As houses become smaller, they are more comfortable if rooms can remain open to each other through elimination of unnecessary walls. In this plan the dining and living areas are separated only by the wood-burning stove. Forming a balcony by extending the walls for those two rooms also gives a feeling of extended space.

10 FEET   NORTH

Diagonal-Roof Home Two 2200 square feet

In severe climates with limited winter sunlight and tricky soil conditions, energy savings must come from insulation and an efficient heat source. Only the main living area in this home has a large window, but a clerestory window allows daylight to spread throughout the house through insulated glass or fiberglass panels. Although heating is more difficult with a two-story living room, the open feeling is helpful in avoiding "cabin fever" during long dark winters.

The front entry can be closed off as a vestibule, with access to a guest bath for changing clothes or washing up after coming in out of the snow.

The kitchen is located between the dining and family rooms rather than out of all the activity so that someone working in the kitchen can still talk with another person in the living room. One objective of this design is to connect all areas so that none will seem cut off from the others. Of course, a few quiet retreats are also needed.

The wood-burning stove is near the stairway so that heat will rise by convection to the upper rooms and a small loft.

The window in the corner of the living room should be triple glazed in view areas and could be made of translucent insulated panels in areas that are exposed to storm winds.

Upstairs, a double bedroom can be divided into two separate bedrooms, then later turned into a large study and guest room after the kids move out. The triangular projection near the loft space reflects light into the upper corridor and protects the doorway below.

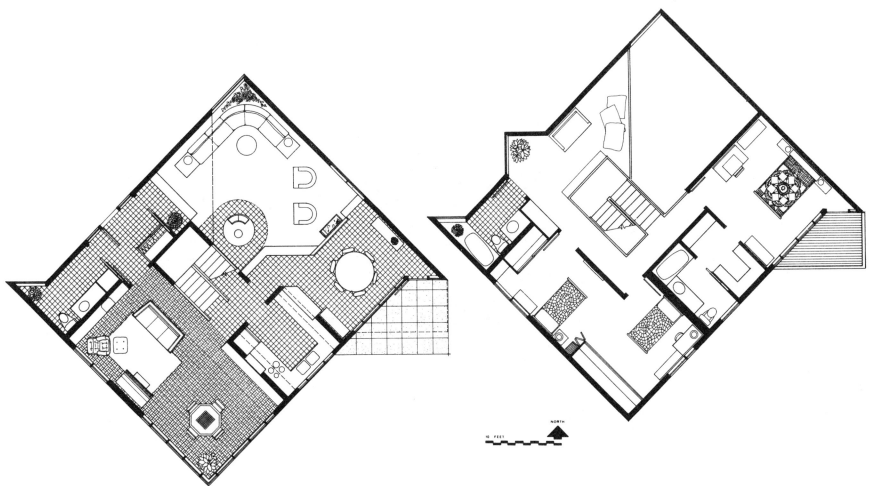

NORTH

10 FEET

This home and the next show two different ways additions could enlarge a simple house typical of many rural areas. Diagrams of these two homes follow on pages 32 and 33.

Both examples are for homes in severely windy climates where heavy insulation is a prime concern. One basic strategy is to attach new areas in a way that further shelters the existing house. This saves extensive changes to walls as the addition becomes the new exterior. Here an existing roof is extended to cover a new bedroom. This is possible because the floor of the new room is several feet lower than the existing floor. With increased insulation and earth berming, the result is more space but lower energy consumption. Since the bathroom window is eliminated, mechanical ventilation must be added.

Within the existing house (shown with unshaded walls), the kitchen is extended to include the former dining area, and the former living room becomes the dining room.

The large addition includes a new entry and the living room/family room combination. Off the kitchen, a utility room is also added. The curved glass wall is oriented to take maximum advantage of afternoon winter sunshine. The rest of the south wall is bermed for shelter from the wind.

Upstairs a loft was created; rising warm air will keep this area quite comfortable for play or craft activities.

The rounding of the exterior of the addition helps blend the house into the surrounding rolling hills and provides a visual contrast with the original form.

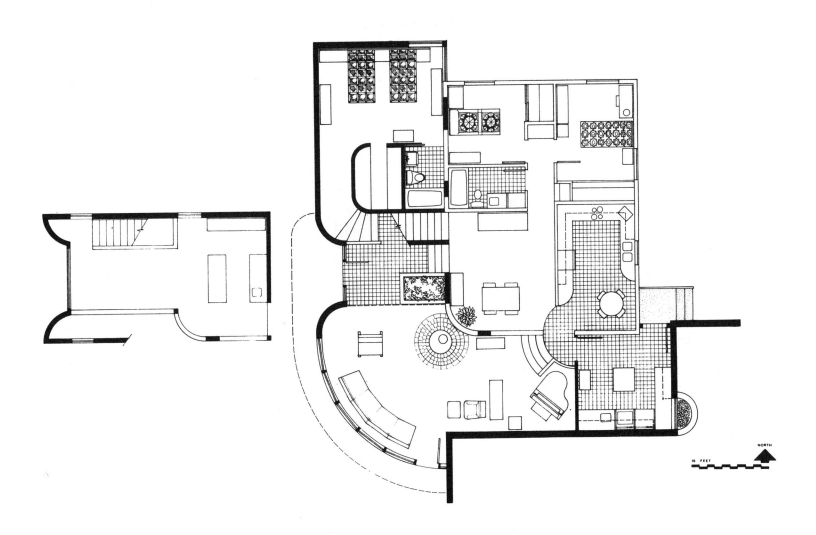

NORTH

10 FEET

Country Home Addition Two 1850 square feet Addition

Often when a home owner builds an addition by himself, the work tends to go on forever. A practical way to reduce the disruption and to break the project down into smaller segments is to do the job in phases. In this house there could be four or more phases, with priorities based on personal preference.

The southern addition is a combination living room and den adjacent to a large greenhouse. This type of greenhouse can store a large amount of heat but is also useful for starting garden plants. A vent in the heat-storing wall near the wood-burning stove allows heat from the stove to warm the greenhouse on cold nights. High windows above the greenhouse let light and heat into the central areas of the house, and they can be opened or covered independently from the greenhouse. This extends the variety of ways the house can be adjusted to changing climatic conditions.

The addition overlaps the existing house enough to hide the connection and to create a small entry. Narrow greenhouses are added along each side of the house to provide a temperature buffer and a variety of spaces for growing plants. They also provide a foreground view for existing rooms. In planning this type of addition, ventilation and emergency fire exiting must be worked out and approved by local building authorities.

A central walkway starts at the greenhouse and continues to the bedroom addition. The last part of the hallway was formerly a closet. The bedroom addition includes the master bedroom, closet, and bath. The addition of a wood-burning stove at this end of the house makes it possible to maintain a comfortable temperature throughout the home without outside power.

A circular stair leads to a loft that can accommodate guests or hobby activities, or provide a play space. These higher areas must include adequate ventilation in homes without forced-air heating or they will typically be five to fifteen degrees warmer than lower areas. In this home, warm air gathered at the highest part of the ceiling is circulated to lower areas by a fan.

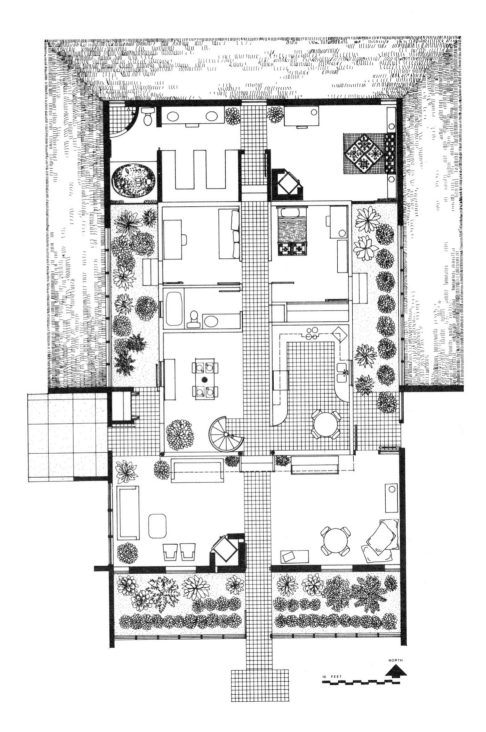

NORTH

10 FEET

Two different additions for the same style house.

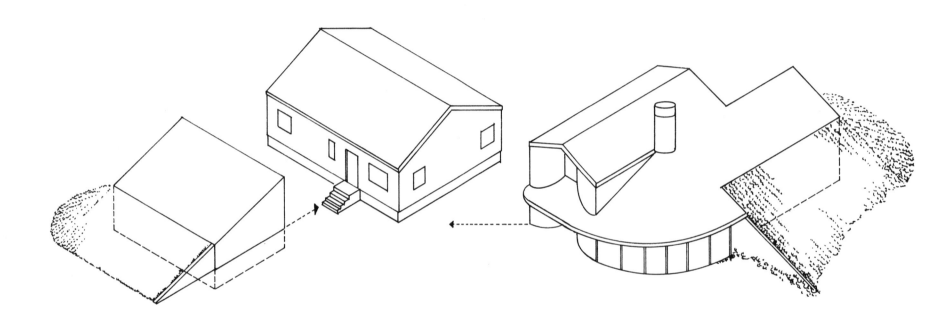

This addition in two parts (see page 28) provides an earth-sheltered master bedroom which helps shelter the existing house. The larger living area addition has rounded forms to completely change the visual image of the home—to not just look like an addition.

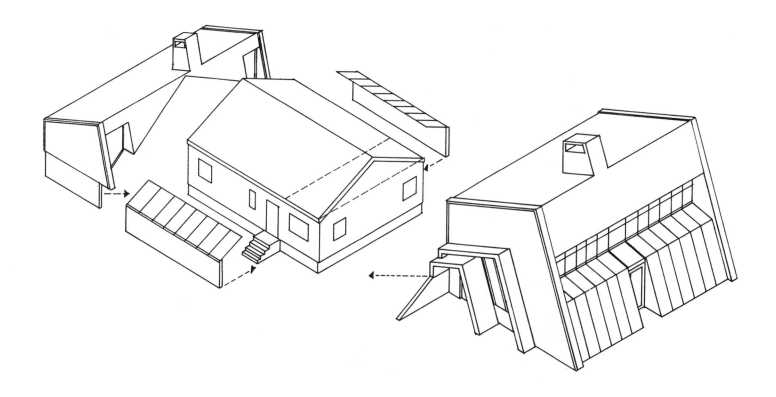

As an alternative, this addition completely surrounds the house with a bedroom addition and three greenhouses. (see page 30).

There was a time when people would look for a "special place" to build their home instead of an "appropriate environment." Despite changes in the way we talk about things, there are still very important reasons why each part of the world is unique. Throughout history we find that every aspect of geographic location—climate, terrain, customs, and politics— has had an influence on building design.

Throughout history we find that every aspect of geographic location—climate, terrain, customs, and politics—has had an influence on building design.

Southwestern adobes, Cape Cod cottages, and prairie houses are all styles that grew out of a need to live with nature in a particular region. We need to design homes for today that both save energy and help us enjoy living in a particular area. Even a suburban lot can be an interesting setting for a home in tune with nature when handled with awareness.

36 A good deal of help is available when it comes to selecting a site or determining the best use of a selected lot. In addition to the expertise provided by consultants such as soil engineers and landscape architects, most localities have free services available through county agencies. A phone call or visit to agency offices is enough to obtain lists of plants

cement trucks could only carry half a load up to the site without spilling. This doubled the number of trips and the cost for installing the concrete (see sketch A).

The shape of the site affects the comfort and the safety of the occupants in many ways. These

gravity breezes at night (see sketch B). A site for another client was the only area for acres where there were no woodchuck holes and the bushes were smaller than average. This clue helped us realize that the mound in the middle of the site was a thinly covered rock, which would have made construction of an earth-sheltered house difficult and

sketch A

sketch B

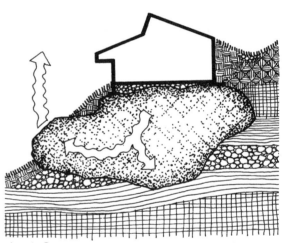

sketch C

that grow well in your area, a general idea about soil and water conditions, or information about regulations that may affect your project. Advice and printed summaries of climate records are available from U.S. Weather Bureau offices.

When you're actually on the site, there are many factors to consider. The first is whether or not construction vehicles can reach the spot selected for your site. One house cost more to build because

effects do not end at the property line. In valleys it's a good idea to check local maps for flood-plain boundaries. This can influence both what you can build and whether or not you can obtain insurance. One client took me to the protected basin on a mountain slope where he hoped to build. The location was beautiful but presented problems. It was directly in line with a large ravine just out of sight on the neighbor's property. It could have been a source of annual floods, and it was the channel for cold

would have drawn heat out from under the house. The mass of the rock kept that part of the ground colder all winter and drier in the summer (see sketch C).

Often soil types change below the surface of the ground to produce a sandwich of problem soils. A six-inch layer of topsoil may hide two feet of expanding clay on top of a water-saturated layer of gravel. The importance of soil layering depends on the type of house you plan to build. One site that could have been a problem for a subsurface house worked out quite well for a home that was bermed up. Twelve feet below the surface, a layer of gravel was the location of a subterranean stream. However, soil tests showed that the bearing was adequate, and the stream, which stayed at fifty-five

Plants also indicate changing soil conditions. If the plant type changes from grasses to dark broad-leafed plants, there is probably a source of water just below the surface. Sometimes the only clue is a sprinkling of wildflowers that show up briefly in the spring. When in doubt, dig a trench and take a look.

and open sites cool and heat very quickly when compared to damp and wooded sites. This will put a more dynamic temperature load on a house. For example, a home on a gently sloping site just into the woods is usually easier to keep comfortable than one only a hundred feet away in a dry flat field or near paved areas (see sketch F).

37

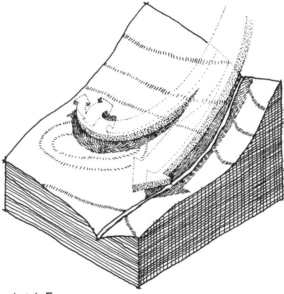

sketch E

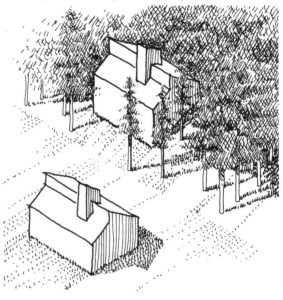

sketch F

sketch D

degrees all year, became the source of almost free heating and cooling from a water-to-air heat pump.

There are far too many examples of lots being sold in the mountains in the paths of recurrent landslides or avalanches. It is always worth comparing the trees on your site with those nearby for size and age. When checking trees, look at the lower section of the trunk. If it curves, there is a good chance you're dealing with some "fast-moving real estate" (see sketch D).

Land form also determines airflow. When there is not a stronger weather pattern, air will generally work its way slowly uphill during the day and then flow down the valleys at night. Areas that are lower than their surrounds will become settling points for cool air—as much as fifteen degrees cooler than areas on nearby slopes (see sketch E).

Exposure and the moisture content of the soil will also affect the heating and cooling of a site. Dry

38   Many books currently available explain how to maximize solar exposure on December 21 and to maximize shade on June 21, but it is not always enough to design for extremes. It's advisable to use more complete sun-angle tables, charts, or computer programs that allow you to fully adapt a design to a specific site.

It may be desirable to you to receive maximum sunlight in the morning every day of the year. This is nice for breakfast areas and for bedrooms for people who need the light to help wake them up. This obviously leads to the use of eastern exposures and window arrangements. Many designs work better if the primary exposure is to the southeast rather than

sketch G

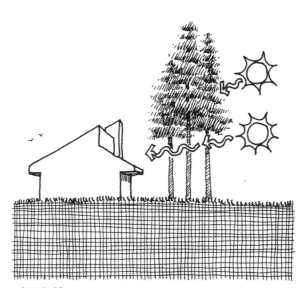

sketch H

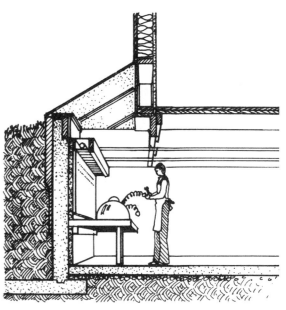

sketch I

If your site is near a hill, a mountain, tall trees, or adjacent buildings, direct sunlight may not reach your site for periods of time (see sketch G). This can be advantageous if western sun is diminished or if the lower branches of a tree can be removed to admit winter sunshine only (see sketch H). One site a client considered purchasing was below the north face of a dramatic cliff. The setting was beautiful in the middle of a summer day, but received no direct sunlight at all for two months in the winter!

to the south. This allows for collection of heat early in the day and easier shading in the late afternoon.

For work areas that need no direct light, diffused light from the north can provide the most uniform natural light. This is particularly useful in hot desert areas. Several skylight materials now provide good light passage along with some insulation value (see sketch I).

Changing light through windows is also useful for special effects. On one home, a window added near a loft to provide an emergency exit was filled with stained glass. Colored light passing through the window streaked across the upper walls at a different time and angle at the end of each day. Faceted, prismatic, or scored glass also produces special effects.

in the roof or walls have advantages over skylights because they are more protected and controllable. They are also good locations for ventilation openings. Skylights take in direct light and heat most of the day and are exposed directly to the cold sky at night. They also usually require special framing in the roof. Despite difficulties, sometimes a skylight is

shows a skylight installation that controls some of the sunlight, requires less special framing, and can be insulated at night (see sketch K).

Ceiling joists were painted white for light diffusion and were allowed to continue through the opening.

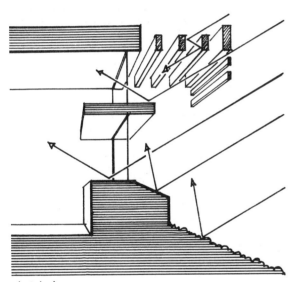

sketch J

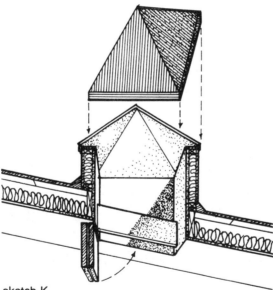

sketch K

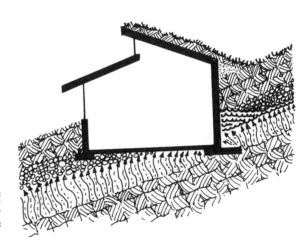

sketch L

When a view of the bright sky is framed by dark or shaded materials, the contrast produces uncomfortable glare. This problem can be minimized by reflecting light onto the soffit (bottom) of the overhang, using a trellis shade, or installing a light shelf (see sketch J). Used carefully, these devices can reflect light farther into the room.

Light is brought still deeper into the room with skylights or clerestories (high windows). High windows

exactly what's needed in a small area like a corridor or shower. In all but the mildest climates, it's usually cost effective to use double glazing to minimize heat gain or loss and condensation. Where a view of the sky is not needed, insulated translucent products are recommended. For smaller sizes (four feet square or less) single-piece units are the least susceptible to leakage and other problems. High-quality larger units using several panes and framing members are also quite reliable now. The illustration

In this case, insulated shutters hang down when the skylight is open and are closed at night. A sliding cover would also work. It is best to not seal these units too tightly from below or damage can be caused by heat build-up. The half-pyramid reflector on top is open to the south in the winter and to the north in the summer.

40

In the mid-1970s earth sheltering received a lot of national attention as a solution to the problem of saving energy. Work on earth-sheltered homes had gone on for several decades, so publications from reliable sources such as the Underground Space Center in Minnesota provided background for experimentation across the country. Home builders had a

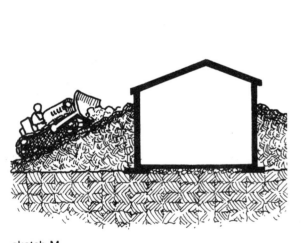

sketch M

negative reaction to many of the early boxlike structures, which resembled gun emplacements. Often the advantages of earth sheltering were overlooked because it was thought that underground housing was limited in style. By working with a variety of clients interested in earth-sheltered homes, architects learned that many options existed in design. To show more people the number of possibilities, *Homes in the Earth* was published. This book showed some of my firm's first earth-sheltered houses

and proposals for others. As we worked with more clients, the variety of designs continued to expand.

Rather than restate the principles of earth sheltering, which are well covered elsewhere, it seems more useful here to share some of the practical lessons I have learned from actual projects.

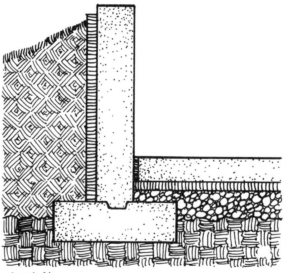

sketch N

There is more than one kind of soil, and one site can include several types. Layered soils increase the chances of underground water, movement, and expansion and contraction (see sketch L).

Occasionally a site has a subsurface rock layer. If the rock is low enough it may be useful as stable bearing. If the rock is exposed to the weather, however, it may draw heat from underneath the house (see sketch C).

With so many possible soil combinations, it is often worth the cost to have a soil test done on potential building sites. The most trouble-free solution is to build on a level, well-drained site and bring in suitable fill for mounds. On one house of this type, as mentioned earlier, soil to be used for mounding was left spread out on the site until the end of a hot August day. When it was pushed into place, the soil was warm enough to avoid the initial energy loss these homes usually experience while bringing surrounding soil up to a stable temperature (see sketch M).

In most northern states, structural foundations need to extend about three feet below the surface to avoid frost heave (shifting of the soil as the ground freezes and expands). When soil conditions permit, foundations can be placed near the surface and a low wall can support a mound above them. This can save up to three feet of wall material (see sketch N).

Soil in the ground or against a wall has much different temperature characteristics than soil "suspended" on a roof. An earth roof is really detached from the soil and is more directly heated by the house below. In most soils the surface temperature is similar to the air temperature although it fluctuates more slowly. With increasing depth the temperature becomes more constant, until at about ten feet below the surface it stabilizes at around fifty-five degrees in the northern states and seventy or more in the South. In most cases, earth-sheltered walls experience less energy loss than walls exposed to air temperatures and wind.

Although earth on the roof can help solve a number of problems such as rapid air temperature change and noise, it creates other problems. First, it is very heavy—from 80 to 150 pounds per cubic foot before it gets wet. That means that a three-foot-deep earth covering may add about 400 pounds per square foot to the roof load!

Second, if the earth on the roof is heated from below, any plants growing on the roof will not have their roots exposed as early to seasonal temperature changes. This can delay dormancy and the plants will die in the first severe freeze. Insulation can minimize this risk, but then the soil can cool to freezing and put more stress on the roofing material. Both problems can be solved if high-quality insulation and roofing products are used.

Some engineers suggest that in some locations earth on the roof doesn't save enough energy to justify the cost. For example, in areas with rainy spring weather earth on the roof doesn't warm as fast as outside air temperatures and thus has a short-term negative effect.

Waterproofing of earth-sheltered homes can be handled very successfully but it can also be a source of difficulties. It is important to think of the combined effect of structural materials, insulation, waterproofing, and soil profile rather than of just the coating or membrane. Concrete and masonry are not usually waterproof by themselves. They're so porous, in fact, that they act like sponges. Post-tensioned concrete, which contains reinforcing rods that are tightened after the concrete hardens, can be waterproof without other treatment. Due to the limited number of shapes that can be created with this method, and the cost of installation, however, this kind of construction is not usually used. Like many methods, it is good if used properly and under the right conditions.

Waterproofing is also a vapor barrier, and it can trap moisture from condensation. This is a problem with insulation that is sprayed on the outside of a concrete wall and then coated with waterproofing. Warm moist air from the interior works its way into the insulation and cools. The moisture condenses on the cool surfaces and either dissolves adhesives

on the wall, freezes and separates layers, or saturates the insulation and reduces its effectiveness. A moisture barrier inside the concrete wall eliminates this problem (see sketch O).

Some membrane roofings that are applied as a liquid offer the advantage of being very stretchable.

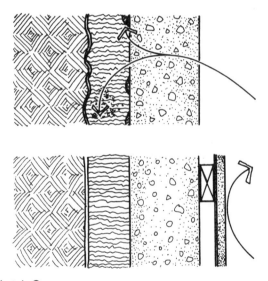

sketch O

Even this has caused some misuse. On plywood roofs, coatings have been used that could stretch up to ten times their original length. Unfortunately, the plywood was shoved together with no space at the joints. As the plywood shrank, the gaps at the joints grew to almost ¼ inch. Although that seems small, it is infinitely larger than no gap at all. This problem is cured by placing bond-breaking tape over joints and spreading out the area that needs to stretch (see sketch P).

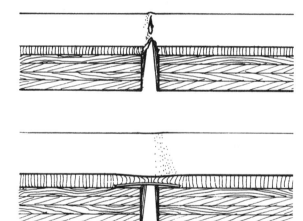

sketch P

On the following two pages, an illustration and checklist combine as a review of considerations in site selection.

Checklist for Site Selection

Access

1. Who owns and maintains the roads to your site? Can you reach the site year-round in all weather?

2. Can emergency vehicles reach your site? How long would it take an ambulance or fire truck to reach your home?

3. Who else uses the road to your site? Will they create problems of noise or dust?

4. Can heavily loaded construction vehicles reach the building area? Would extra trips or charges be involved?

5. What utilities are available to your site? What provisions must be made for power outages?

6. How easy is it to reach other points of interest in the area from this site? Where would you go for schools, shopping, mail delivery, and other needs?

7. How will future development change the area?

8. What are the neighbors like?

9. What governmental agencies have jurisdiction over your area for development and building codes? What can they tell you about your site?

10. Do you like the view from your site? What can be done to improve the view without damaging the site?

11. How will your home look from other areas on and off the site? Will it be hidden or will it attract visitors?

12. What problems might parking vehicles cause?

Weather

13. What is the climate of your area and how does it differ from what you're accustomed to? How will it affect home design?

14. How much sunlight is the site totally exposed to during the warm months? How much sunlight is cut off by hills, mountains, or adjacent structures?

15. How much sunlight is available during colder months?

16. What effect do trees have on available sunlight? Will this change as the trees grow taller or are removed?

17. How will daily airflow patterns influence comfort? Will cool downhill breezes leave pockets of cold air? How exposed is the site to breezes for ventilation?

18. What else is in the air? Are you in the take-off zone for a nearby airport?

19. Can local breezes carry industrial pollutants, odors, dust, or possible radioactive contamination?

20. What measures can be taken to protect the property from range or forest fires?

21. Do storms carrying rain, snow, or high winds come from the same direction as other winds?

22. How could severe weather alter the site (landslides, snowslides, fallen trees, snow drifts, surface water)?

Soil and Water

23. Is the bearing capacity of the soil adequate for the type of construction you have in mind? What are the soil types and how do they affect site use?

24. Is ground water a problem on this site? How does it vary during the year? Is it a potential heating or cooling source?

25. Is drinking water available? How deep are the wells in the area? How much will a well probably cost?

26. Is there appropriate room for other uses of the site without interfering with the home site? These could include workshops, storage, gardens, or keeping animals.

27. Will you be sharing the site with burrowing or dam-building animals? What can their activities tell you about the site?

28. Are there stagnant ponds, marshes, or other nearby sources of insect pests?

29. Is there a potential for flooding either in a broad flood plain or a local channel? Will this affect your ability to get a building permit or insurance? Can the site be protected at reasonable expense?

30. Can subsurface rock that is exposed elsewhere carry heat away from the house?

31. What earthquake zone is this house in, and how would local soils and site features be affected by an earthquake?

43

Split-Greenhouse Home 2850 square feet

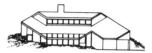

44

This residence is an example of a home designed to reflect the client's interests in computer technology, art, and the natural environment. It was designed for a rural site near a city in the semi-desert region of Washington state. Although it is designed to save energy, it does so through the application of new technology rather than a reliance on old-fashioned methods. It's a rural lifestyle that does not turn away from progress.

Most unusual in the plan is a split greenhouse. Earlier projects with large greenhouses had demonstrated that, except in the coldest months, full solar heat collection was excessive. Rather than use a smaller greenhouse, which would have been inadequate in January and February, a central wall was added to form two greenhouses side by side. While one side is being used for heat collection, the other side can be open to the living room for additional seating space.

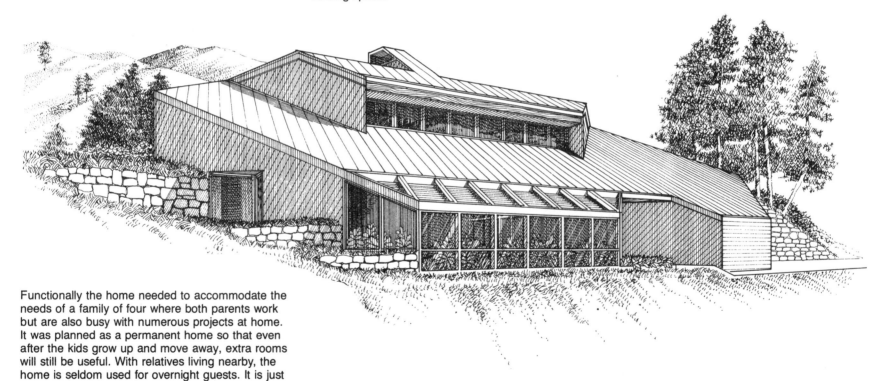

Functionally the home needed to accommodate the needs of a family of four where both parents work but are also busy with numerous projects at home. It was planned as a permanent home so that even after the kids grow up and move away, extra rooms will still be useful. With relatives living nearby, the home is seldom used for overnight guests. It is just remote enough to be affected by occasional power failures and closed roads, so it must be somewhat self-sufficient for short periods of time.

The diagram to the right was included in the working drawings to give the owner an overall view of construction. It is preferable to have a professional builder construct custom homes to take advantage of his expertise. If the owner wishes to build his own home to save money or for the adventure of doing it himself, he must realize that it is a very big job and may take much longer than he imagined. It can also lead to a great sense of accomplishment.

Most of these homes are assembled using common construction practices. Much of the concrete work is similar to that for a typical basement wall, although it may be more heavily reinforced in some areas. The shorter retaining walls at the front of the house are like normal footings, except the floor is near the bottom of the footing rather than near the top. The result is a shorter stud wall above.

Above the concrete wall, construction is a normal frame wall, usually two-by-sixes to provide enough depth for insulation. Walls are usually insulated to values of R-20 and ceilings to R-38 (these are the standard insulation values for walls and ceilings). Heavily insulated roofs are particularly important where there is no attic as an additional temperature buffer.

Interior walls near the stove/fireplace and areas exposed to winter sunlight are made of concrete block for heat storage.

Staying as close as possible to standard details on the greenhouse can also save a lot of time and money.

The project architect for this home was Don Green.

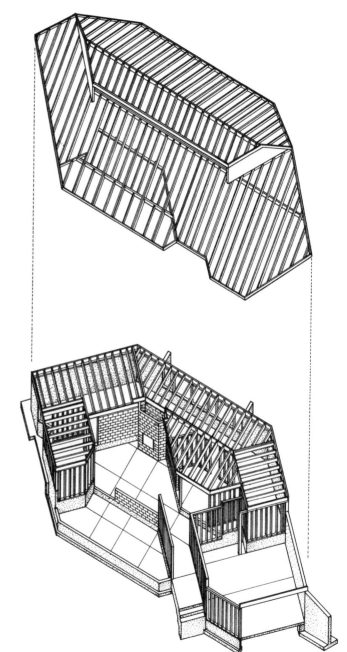

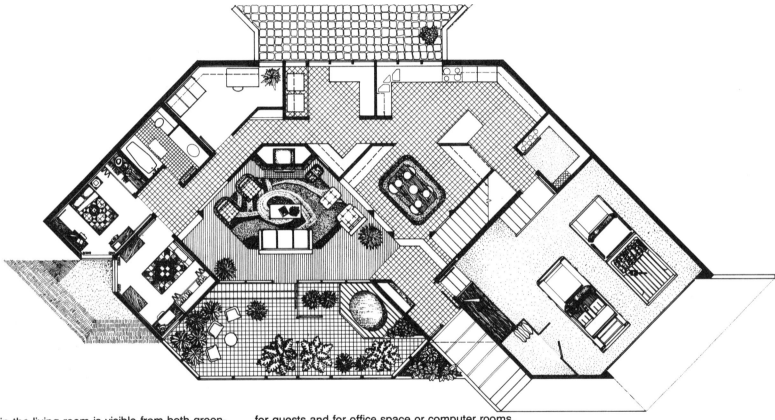

Activity in the living room is visible from both green-houses, the dining room, the hallway, and the master bedroom. This creates a very open feeling in the house without giving up privacy where it is needed. One factor in providing so much wall area in the living room was the need for adequate display areas for artworks.

Two main-floor bedrooms and a bath form a domain for the children. Eventually these rooms will be used for guests and for office space or computer rooms. Along the back wall is an office, a work/crafts area, an expanded kitchen with a baking center, an insulated pantry that remains at ground temperature, and the garage. The back wall has planted earth mounds up to the eaves, but the mounds dip below window level in the middle. This allows a view out the back and a shortcut for passing firewood into the house (and into a two-sided storage cabinet in the workroom that opens to the living room).

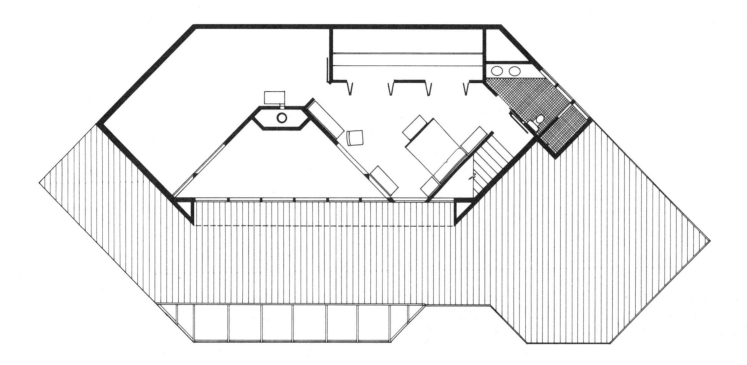

Upstairs, the master bedroom has a view from the balcony into the living room, a high view to the southern sky and hilltops, and a view through the bath to the hills to the north.

In addition to the furnace/storage room there is an area above the kids' bedrooms that can become a loft.

After this house had been designed, another client saw the design and thought it would be close to what he needed. The concept for the floor plan remained although it was enlarged somewhat, and materials were changed to be more appropriate to his site near Fresno, California. (See the Side-Greenhouse Home, page 50.)

A wood floor above a rock heat-storage area was considered originally. This has provided attractive and comfortable floors in other homes. After studying initial and long-range costs and energy efficiency, it was decided instead to use a concrete floor poured directly on gravel, with air circulation tubes below and carpet on top in areas that don't receive direct sunlight.

Based on the combined use of the greenhouse, insulation, and earth sheltering, a computer estimate was made of the electrical consumption necessary for heating this house; the amount was about 10 percent of the requirement for similarly sized older conventional homes in the area. Using a wood-burning stove for emergency backup and supplemental heating could eliminate the need for electrical heat.

In the two-story living room, a curved white-stained wood ceiling evenly diffuses sunlight that has been reflected from the roof through the high window. The roof color is important because it will be reflected into the house. White or blue or even silver roofs would work, although a light wheat color is used here to blend the house into the site. Dark colors would have little reflection, and red or green colors could produce undesirable lighting effects.

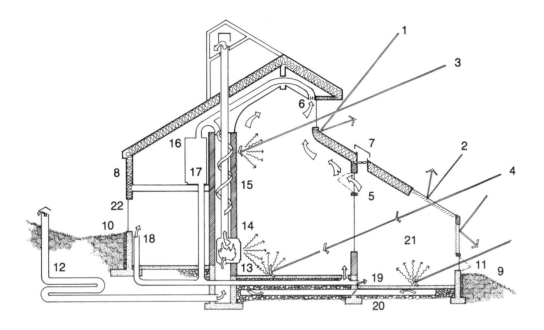

Many methods of saving energy, such as using less hot water and setting the thermostat a few degrees lower in the winter, are adjustments to lifestyle rather than to buildings. Other minor details such as weatherstripping and the use of good sealants in construction joints can account for a large reduction of heat loss due to air infiltration. This diagram shows many other devices and methods that will also save energy. The success of any of these depends on how well they are combined with other means of energy conservation.

1. Summer sun is kept out of the house by overhangs at windows.
2. Summer sun is reflected away by light-colored blinds.
3. Winter sun shines through windows and heats concrete blocks.
4. Winter sun shines through windows and heats tile and concrete floors.
5. Operable windows or vents allow warm air from the greenhouse to rise into the main living area.
6. Air warmed by several sources in the house rises to a vent near the highest part of the ceiling to be collected for recirculation.
7. Excess heat is exhausted from the greenhouse. Usually this fan unit is controlled by a thermostat.
8. The walls, the roof, and below-grade areas are insulated.
9. Where windows aren't needed, dirt mounds are placed against exterior walls.

10. Where the house is built into an existing hillside the land is reshaped to promote drainage of rain or melting snow.
11. Operable windows are arranged to take advantage of natural ventilation.
12. A long underground tube—50 to 150 feet of one-foot diameter pipe—is used to temper air being supplied to the air-circulation unit. Usually this cools air enough to eliminate the need for air conditioning in northern states and coastal areas. In winter the air is warmed before reaching the furnace.
13. Some of the outside air is used by the wood-burning stove. Otherwise air would be taken from the interior of the house, causing cold outside air to be drawn into living areas.
14. An airtight stove burns wood efficiently and radiates heat to the main living area.
15. Outside air is warmed by flowing around the stove and flue before being circulated in the house.

16. Warmed outside air is combined with collected warm air from the ceiling vent and is blown through the house again after filtration.
17. An efficient heat-pump system moves heat from an exterior air or water source to heat interior air when other sources are inadequate or not in use.
18. Heated air is delivered at the base of windows to minimize drafts.
19. During extreme cold spells some warm air is released to the greenhouse.
20. Air tubes in a gravel bed beneath the floor help equalize floor temperatures.
21. The split greenhouse is described earlier.
22. Windows are double glazed, with thermal breaks in any metal parts, or wood frames are used. Wood frames must be weatherstripped and sealed to prevent the infiltration of air.

Side-Greenhouse Home 2650 square feet

This house illustrates what can happen when an existing house plan is chosen for use with just a few changes. It started out as the preceding split-greenhouse home. Instead of being built in Washington, though, it was to be built in central California. The house was also approached from a busy street on the west rather than a drive from the east, and the plan needed to be larger. Next, the greenhouse didn't need to be so large but the kitchen had to be larger. Once those items were resolved, materials were changed to suit the climate, and a patio was added in back, there were only stylistic similarities to the original concept!

The client felt that a house couldn't be built in California without a hot tub. When the client for the Washington house saw this plan, though, he decided to add a hot tub to his plan, too!

One item that doesn't show on the plan is an underground tube about one hundred feet long to moderate the temperature of outside air brought in for ventilation. There is still inadequate data on the effectiveness of this device, but the owner of this house was interested enough to give it a try. It is important to realize that with any of these homes energy-saving is the result of coordinating several

elements, including a greenhouse, mounding, insulation, and shades. These, combined with a judicious use of economizer cycles on the furnace and good maintenance, result in efficient energy conservation.

An extra feature of this plan is a room with a sink and a toilet in the garage for convenience when working in the garage shop and for use as a mudroom after outside activities.

In warm climates it is useful to think about ways in which the shape of the house can be used to create shaded areas outdoors. The north side of this home shades an outdoor patio.

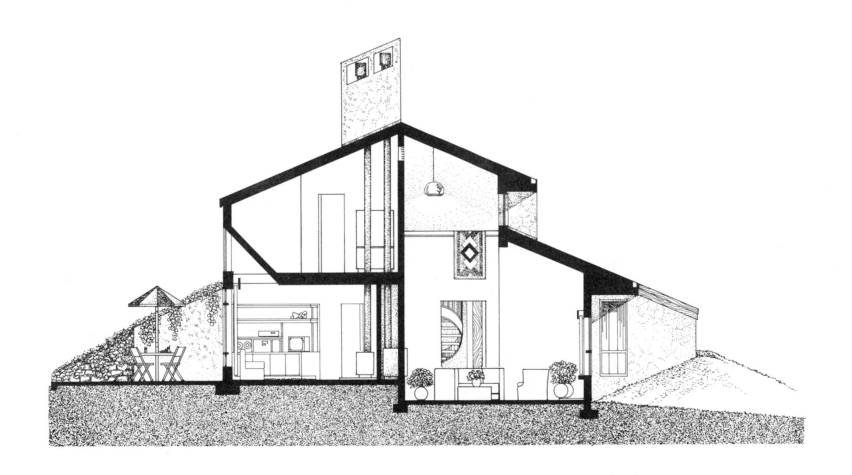

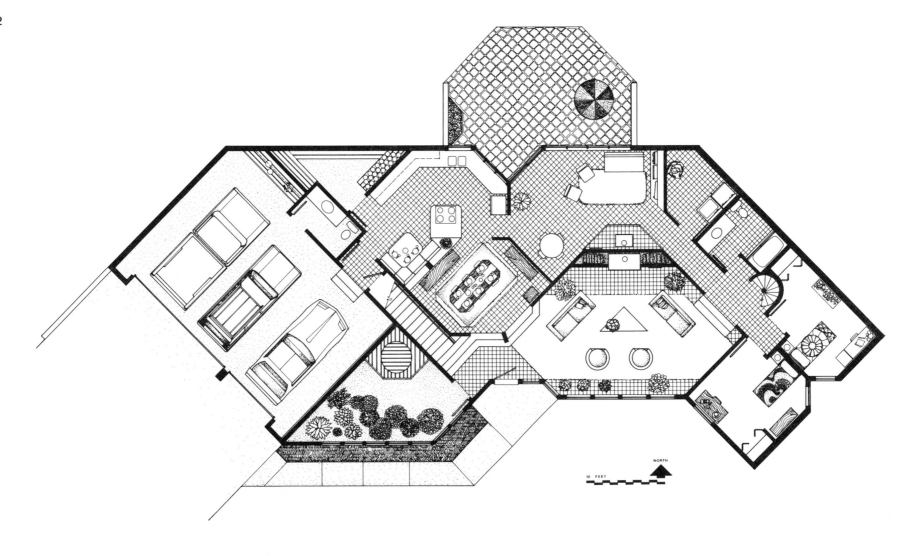

NORTH

10 FEET

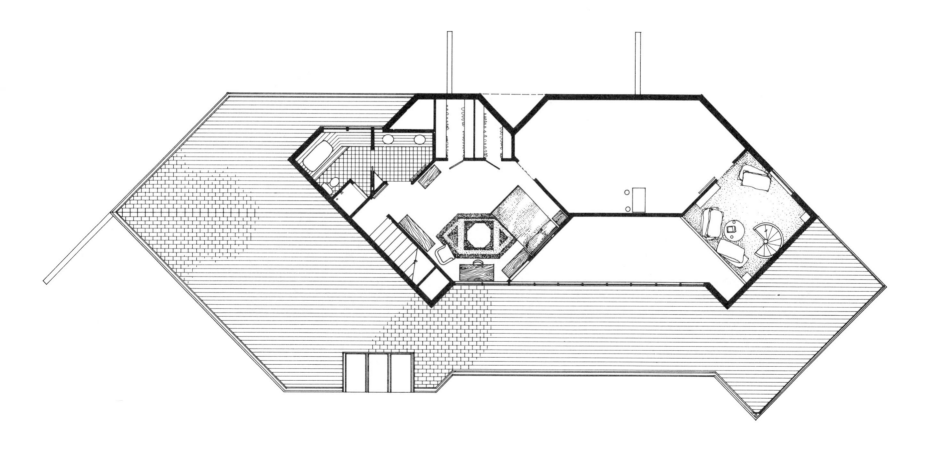

Central Living Room Home 2300 square feet

54   This plan was designed for a couple who decided to retire first and grow old later. Settling in a valley with several of their relatives nearby, they wished to build a home that was a modification to a meadow rather than an object on the land. This energy-efficient home makes a very soft visual impression.

A large deck is provided for outdoor activities and for observing nature. A house like this is so integrally tied to nature that the quiet chirping of crickets in the evening is worth taking time for.

This home was designed in collaboration with architect Don Green of Spokane, Washington.

With much of the view to the west, several small windows are provided in the bedrooms and the dining area. Overhangs delay full exposure to the sun until late afternoon, and native grasses reduce reflected heat.

A pantry is located in a corner of the garage to take advantage of cool earth temperatures for longterm storage of bulk foods and wine.

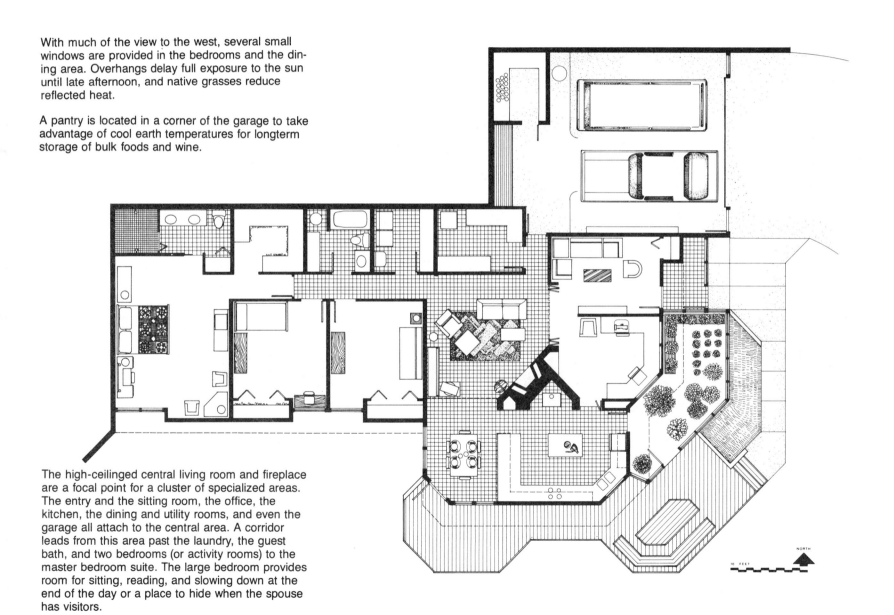

The high-ceilinged central living room and fireplace are a focal point for a cluster of specialized areas. The entry and the sitting room, the office, the kitchen, the dining and utility rooms, and even the garage all attach to the central area. A corridor leads from this area past the laundry, the guest bath, and two bedrooms (or activity rooms) to the master bedroom suite. The large bedroom provides room for sitting, reading, and slowing down at the end of the day or a place to hide when the spouse has visitors.

NORTH

10 FEET

Segmented Home 2690 square feet

In this home, several rooms are linked together to form a chain of activity areas ranging from most public to most private. The plan could easily be modified to add extra bedrooms or rooms for other purposes. Floor levels could also change with each segment to accommodate a sloping site.

From the garage area there is a choice of entering the office area to the right or entering the house through the greenhouse. The size of the greenhouse can vary according to the geographic region and the uses to be made of the room. Warm air from the greenhouse can be distributed throughout the house or it can be used just for growing plants.

The greenhouse, garage, workroom, living room, and corridor all connect with an entry area. There is a built-in bench for changing into outdoor clothes and a storage closet for coats and gear.

The main corridor provides views into the private garden and connects the series of rooms without passing through them. The "quiet" end of the house includes the bedrooms and bathrooms. This area has a sod roof for additional sound isolation from outdoor noises.

The living, dining, and activity rooms have floor-to-ceiling windows for maximum light, views, and winter heat gain. These rooms also have narrow windows in the upper walls. The windows are adjacent to interior walls and filled with colored glass so that colored light streaks across the walls in patterns that vary throughout the day and year. The windows in the bedrooms start three feet above the floor but still provide much light and view.

Radiating walls, decks, and mounds help integrate this house into the site.

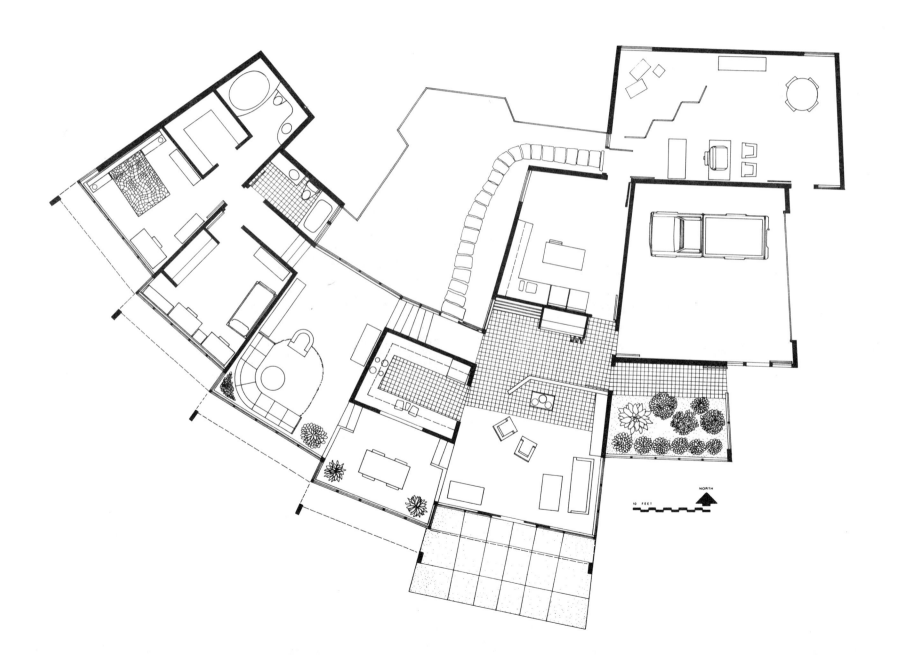

57

NORTH

10 FEET

Fan-Plan Home 2250 square feet

58   The radiating shape of this plan allows each room
to face a different direction. The land also slopes to
the east on this site, so that the house steps down
as it swings from west to east. Entry from the
garage through the utility room is handy to the ·
kitchen at the center of the home. Visitors would
take a short trail around the landscaped mound to
the entry vestibule.

The living room would be particularly enjoyable as it
warms in the morning sun. It would seem like a
"sunken" living room, since it is a few steps down
from the dining area.

The greenhouse absorbs solar heat but also provides a foreground view for the dining and kitchen
areas and frames the view beyond. A deck at this
level provides a convenient outdoor dining area separate from the main activity deck, which is a few
steps up and acts as an extension of the activity
room. The extension of rooms through the use of
decks makes rooms seem larger and more open.
The master bedroom has a more secluded deck for
enjoying a leisurely beginning or ending to the day.

From the activity area, steps lead up to a loft that
overlooks the living room. High windows shaded by
reflective blinds allow heat to be absorbed by back
walls and to make the loft a sunny wintertime
retreat. This ring of high windows also reflects light
down into the bathrooms. In more southern states,
these windows would need a protective overhang.

Additional rooms could be added to this plan until a
complete circle is created.

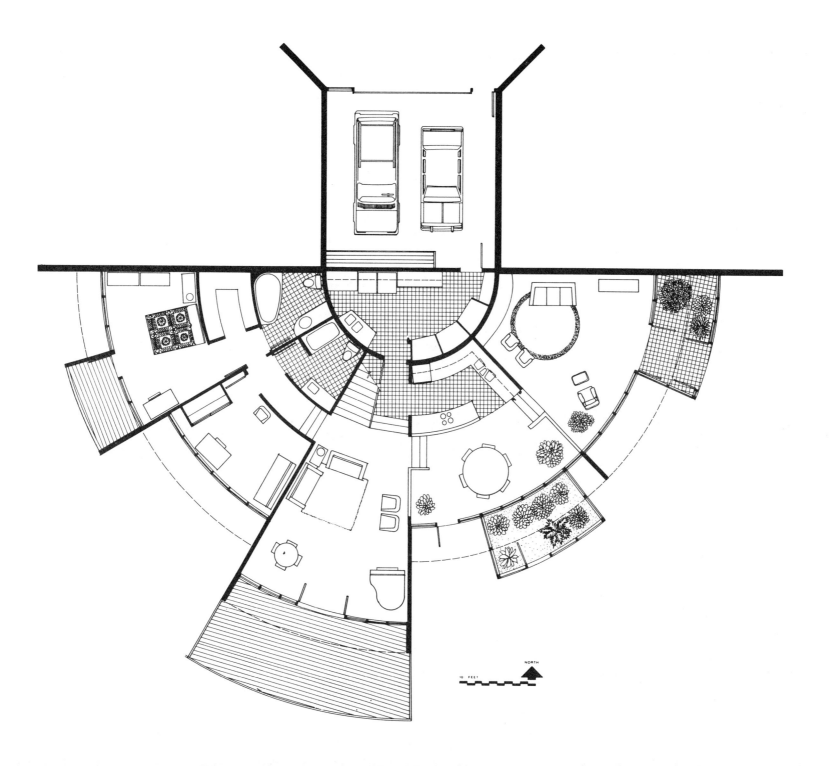

NORTH

10 FEET

Three-Square Pavilion Home 1500 square feet

In this plan, sloping side roofs meet at a pyramid roof topped by a skylight to cover a structure formed by three squares. A half-circle family room extends the plan to the south, and a smaller semicircle creates an entry vestibule on the north side. The central area of the home is divided by a tile walkway from the entry to the family room and by a stairway that leads to a loft above the sitting and utility rooms. High windows in the kitchen and dining areas allow light to reach well into the house.

The west wing has two bedrooms, two baths, and a storage closet. The smaller bedroom could be a study if the house was built for a couple without children, or for a single person.

The semicircular form of the family room allows a wraparound view. Exposure to the sun could be adjusted at different times of the day through varying combinations of window coverings.

The step down from kitchen to family room means that the bar area can be counter height in the kitchen and stool height on the other side. This variation in levels also blocks views of kitchen counters from the family room. A utility room and a pantry are adjacent to the kitchen for convenience.

The result of this design is a home with a wide variety of room shapes, views, and exposures. It provides protection from the environment along with an open and spacious feeling.

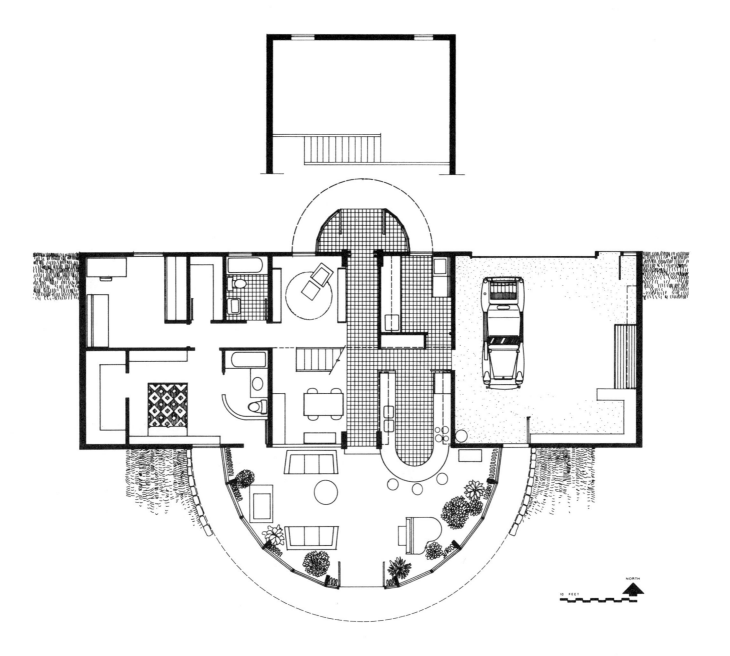

NORTH

10 FEET

Southern-Steps Home 1600 square feet

Flat roofs allow almost any shape of floor plan because roof slopes don't need to be taken into account. Few roofs are actually totally flat because enough slope is necessary to improve drainage, but generally the roof just goes wherever the rest of the house does. Here three pyramid roofs are added above the living room, dining area, and den. Small skylights at the top of each pyramid diffuse light across the sloping ceilings. In hotter climates the south and west sides of the skylights would be reflective or temporarily covered in the summer.

Four rooms along the south side of the house are separated only by steps in the wall. This maintains an open feeling and, for some people, more privacy is not required. Behind the kitchen is a large pantry. Off the master bedroom there is a large bath that includes a therapy tub. A quiet nook off the patio is also adjacent to the bedroom.

The entire north wall has no openings and could be a property wall if no setbacks are required. Outside, a series of small planters reduces the amount of heat reflected from paved areas into the house. Heat pumps could cool the house by transferring heat to the pool.

Placing the small bedroom near the entry provides more privacy for use as a guest room or a child's room. The living room has views of both the yard and a private garden. This garden is also visible from the kitchen and from a shop off the garage.

The floor plan steps from southwest to northeast to allow maximum penetration of morning sunlight and early cut-off of direct sun after noon. The location of the garage and the screen wall near the entry further reduces late-afternoon heat gain.

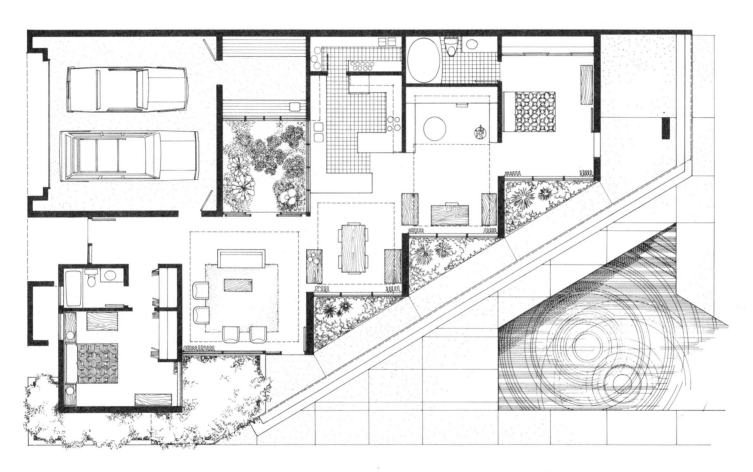

10 FEET

NORTH

Sunspace Home 2450 square feet

64   This plan could be considered a square structure over an "L"-shaped plan. The fourth corner is a two-story greenhouse that acts as an entry, a sun room, and a sitting area for the upper floor. With this much exposure effective shades are required in most climates. Reflective miniblinds between the panes of glass could be very effective if operated remotely and automatically by timer or thermostat. Hot air is collected at the peak of the roof and moved by fan to the rest of the house in the winter. In the summer the air is exhausted to induce natural ventilation.

Bay windows are used at several locations on both floors to reduce visual separation between indoors and outdoors and to increase the apparent size of the rooms. In this house entertaining takes place on the first floor and the upstairs is reserved for family. The master bedroom has a balcony and a view into the sun room.

The rear side walls of the greenhouse could either be a high-mass material, such as masonry, or stud walls with eutectic salt containers built in for heat storage.

In a two-story greenhouse, plants must be arranged vertically as well as horizontally. This requires pulleys or platforms but produces a very dramatic indoor garden.

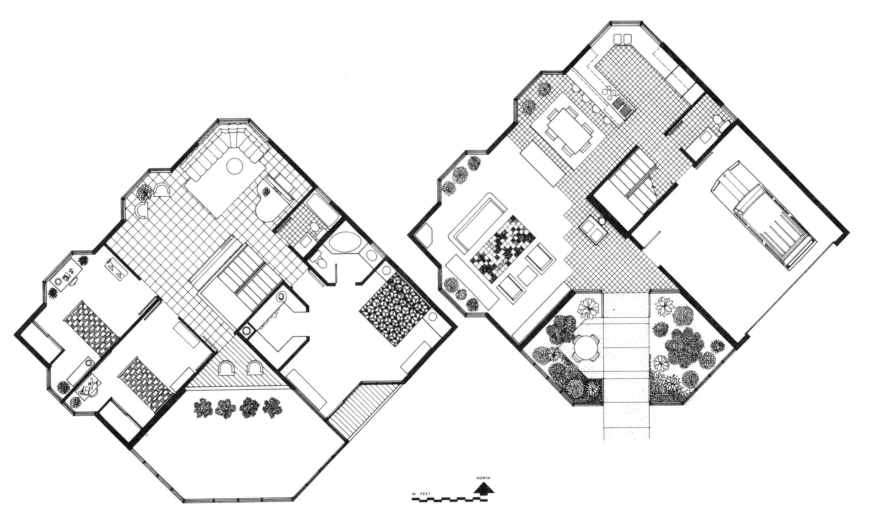

NORTH

10 FEET

Designing for Personal Preference

The functional requirements for a home are seldom so confining that they totally define its appearance. Although special needs or unusual site conditions may lead to a specialized type of construction, the occupant's choices of materials, color, and details allow room for personal expression. Even if you have a very disciplined, stylized, or even stereotyped idea of how your house should look, there is still room for your own unique preferences and your own responses to the time and place in which you

...there is still room for your own unique preferences and your own responses to the time and place in which you live.

live. When we admire a historically significant residence we see in its form and construction much of the story of the lives of the people who first made it a home. Our challenge today is to both learn from our past and yet express our preferences using modern materials and construction methods.

Designing for Personal Preference

Environmental, functional, and technical concerns are brought together under the influence of any particular building style. A style may be indicative of regional history or borrowed from another time and place. It may be an established style such as Colonial, Georgian, English Tudor, or Post-Modern. For some home owners a style may be a personal attempt to create inhabited sculpture. Whatever the case may be, the strongest expression of individualism in architecture is a result of your own combination of personal preferences and responses.

If your choice of home style is limited merely to what is currently popular or frequently constructed, a residence will become just one among many commodities for you to purchase.

Each historical era copies its predecessors with varying degrees of success. Colonial Americans copied earlier European styles and, at worst, ended up with comic collages of palace parts spliced to flimsy wooden cottages in a vain attempt to imply culture. More sophisticated residences, such as Thomas Jefferson's Monticello, blended European tradition with personal ingenuity to form a unique and elegant variation on existing styles.

Even today, if asked for a personal preference, many people will say they like "Early American" architecture. This becomes somewhat vague when we stop to consider the richness and variety of styles from early United States history. The drawing shows not only the familiar "Cape Cod," "Plantation," and "Victorian" styles but also the less familiar "Federalist," "Cape May," and "Romanesque" styles among others that make up a still very incomplete collection of styles from our country's early history. It's also worth remembering that there were several styles of houses already standing when the first Europeans landed on the continent, so a few Native American examples are included.

A major influence in the design of homes is regional style. The development of a style associated with a particular region is the result of climatic influences, the availability of materials, and the local culture. One prominent example is the town of Santa Fe, where buildings are required to conform to a limited palette of materials and colors reminiscent of some of the local homes, which are among the oldest buildings in the country. The result, though somewhat limiting to personal expression, is a pleasant consistency that allows variation within a style and produces a unique community. The bay windows of San Francisco homes and the Oriental influences in Northwest homes are examples of styles developing as responses to local conditions.

Today, increased mobility and mass communication have made every part of the country a melting pot of many cultures. At the same time, advancing technology has made it possible to ignore traditional local materials and use substitutes or imitations to produce styles that have no relevance to an area at all. Although technological advances have led to greater freedom of design, historical precedents still provide starting points for new designs.

Regional design can be incorporated into an otherwise contemporary design through use of traditional materials, details, or colors.

Often it is difficult to separate regional and historical design influences. Santa Fe haciendas and Cape Cod cottages are both historical and regional in origin. The majority of homes, however, are built in areas where dominant styles are less obvious. In these areas it is difficult to adopt a historical style without having design elements look applied, irrelevant, or nostalgic. Even the truly historic precedents in an area may have been inappropriate from the beginning. There are many examples of materials being shipped great distances and local opportunities being totally ignored because of someone's preconception of what a home should be. Many early designs made sense at the time, but others didn't. It is worth studying the heritage of each region to learn how people made decisions about how they could live happily and comfortably in their environment. And as a matter of local pride we can consider incorporating appropriate regional and historical features into our design.

Even though we think of dramatic events and prominent individuals when we think of history, our daily lives may be more influenced by unwritten folk history. The charm of folk arts such as quilting and stenciling soften the hard edges of many homes today. The importance attached to owning land in the past still compels most of us to want at least a small lot with a sometimes useless front yard.

Now, in the era of mass marketing, we are faced with the implication that, with few exceptions, we are all very much alike. Public architecture is often designed for a fictitious "average" person and responds more to the demands of building codes and professional liabilities than to personal needs. The home is becoming the only building type that can still respond to the needs and preferences of individuals or families. No two people can perceive the world exactly the same way even if they try. Each perception is the result of a combination of a unique cultural background, personal experiences, current attitudes and conditions, and neurological structure. People see, hear, feel, and taste in different ways; or they may ignore most of their perceptions by daydreaming about something else. If people are all so different, perhaps their houses should also be unique.

Twin-Octagon Home 3100 square feet

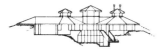

70   Residences become more interesting and personal when they reflect the values and traditions of their owners. The house shown in this example is similar to a house built in wheat country in southeastern Washington state. In addition to fulfilling all of the usual farmhouse functions, the design reflects the octagonal shapes of many of the area's earlier pioneer buildings. These early buildings were assembled from two-by-fours nailed together flat to produce very durable silos and other structures. Interestingly, these faceted buildings were similar in shape and color to the basalt outcroppings of the area.

By using the octagonal form, we produced a design that was functional but also related to the history and land form of the area without copying any outdated details. When a wind vane was added, the octagon shape was repeated for it also.

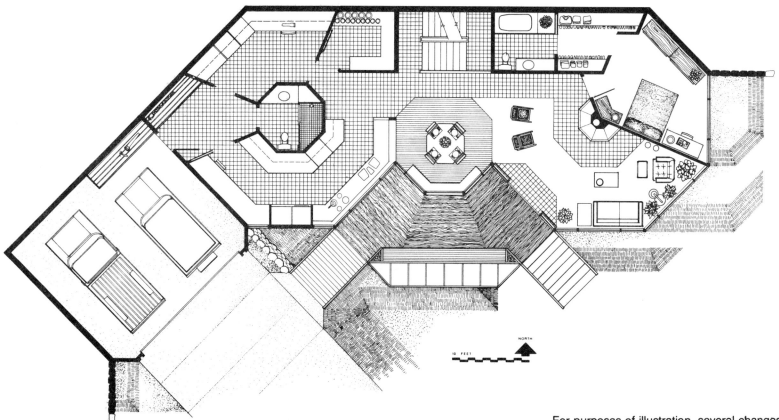

NORTH

10 FEET

For purposes of illustration, several changes have been made to the roof structure and to the floor plan. The actual house has pyramid skylights at the peaks of simpler roofs. This produced a less-expensive solution than the one shown here. The skylights also provided a great place for the family dog to sit to keep warm on cool days after walking up the berm (earth mound) against the back of the house and onto the roof. The truss roof shown here is an alternative.

In this plan, the two octagons form separate activity areas linked by a central stair and a dining area. The east segment contains bedrooms (on two floors), bathrooms, and the living room. The west segment contains the kitchen, pantry, sewing room, mudroom, and office areas. Upstairs a craft room has a view of most of the fields as well as of distant mountains. Downstairs are the bedrooms, a large family room, and a greenhouse. The greenhouse is used for growing out-of-season vegetables and for trapping solar heat. The heat can be allowed to rise directly into the living room and dining area in cooler months. The family room includes a modified vertical version of a Russian fireplace. These fireplaces consist of a large brick mass with a complex flue that allows more heat from the fire to be held within the house rather than passing up the chimney with the smoke.

In this house, traditional forms and devices are combined to form a design that contains many of the elements we value in older homes, and yet the appearance is very modern.

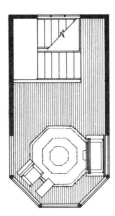

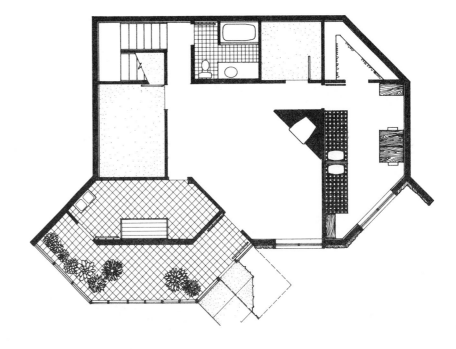

New Mexican Suburban Home 2450 square feet

74 The simple masses, plain walls, and projecting rain scuppers of historic desert Southwest homes are more than just expressions of taste. The massive walls with their minimal windows provide shelter from intense daytime heat and store enough heat to ward off the desert chill at night. Since the walls are made of adobe, it is necessary to project rain water being drained from the roof far enough to avoid washing away the walls.

Despite years of technological advances, many of the principles that made early structures work are still valid. One pleasant alternative for modern design combines traditional design forms with modern windows, fireplaces, insulation, and electronic devices. In this way, a home that tempers the environment with mass heat storage also can be light and open in plan.

The design of this home starts with massive walls. Windows are used only where essential to admit light or frame a view. Planters are used for earth sheltering, and closets are located on outside walls for additional insulation value. South-facing windows have overhangs to cut off direct summer sunlight. They also have "blinders"—projecting walls to the sides of the window—to cut out low-angled sunlight from the east and west. Trellises on the west walls provide additional shade to keep heat off the walls. A wood-burning stove is built into the fireplace to back up the heat pump. On hot days a ceiling fan will improve room air circulation.

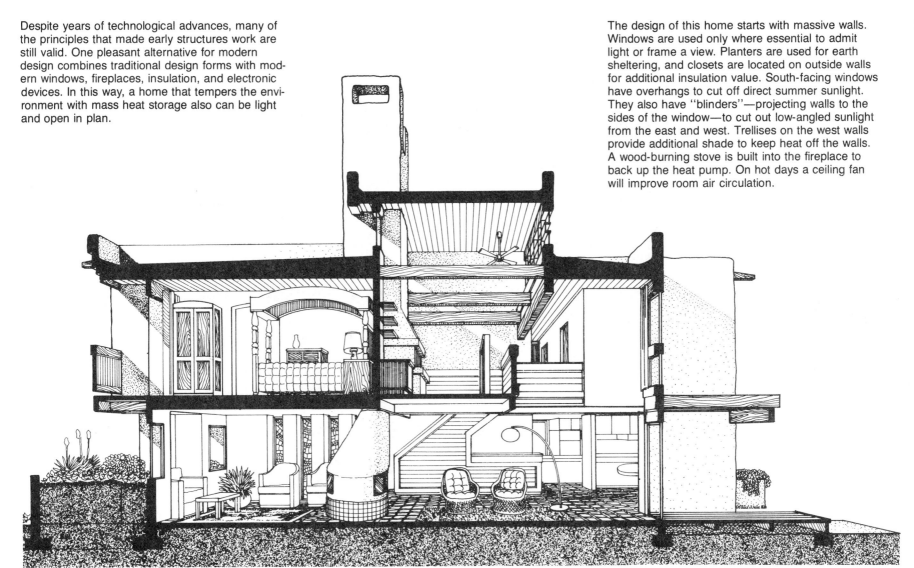

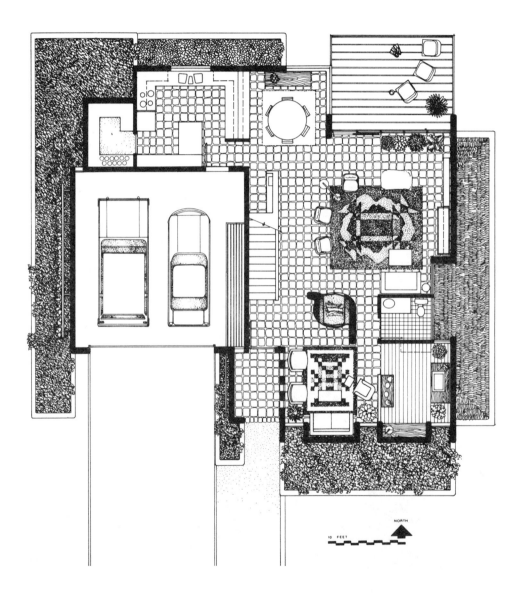

NORTH

10 FEET

The main floor includes a sheltered entry that leads to a conversation area. The fireplace is visible from this room and from the much larger family room. A study and a small bath are also adjacent to the fireplace, positioned so that the study has a view of the fire but the bath is hidden. The dining area and bar (under the stair) are extensions of the family room, so that all rooms can be used at once. Although the plan turns and includes several projections, most areas are visible from most other areas.

A pass-through from the dining room to the kitchen makes the latter less isolated. The kitchen includes a central work table and an adjacent pantry.

Ceiling-to-floor glass on the north side of the family room extends that area visually onto the deck. The view of the backyard further reduces the feeling of enclosure.

All three bedrooms are upstairs, with the children's rooms well separated from the master bedroom. Anyone working in the kitchen can hear the kids jump out of bed in the morning.

The master bedroom has a walk-in closet, a balcony, and a private bath. The balcony provides fresh air and a quiet place to read or just sit on pleasant mornings and evenings. Diffused colored light shines into the master shower and on through a high relite (indoor window) into the bedroom.

Overlooking the family area, the crafts balcony provides an alcove for projects, so that the mess is out of sight but people are not out of touch.

Post-Tyrolean Home 2500 square feet

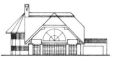

Occasionally an opportunity arises to design a home for a geographical area that has strict design covenants. Some architects will refuse such a commission but others see the situation as a chance to reconsider their esthetic values and to work under a different set of stylistic guidelines. This house was designed for a mountain resort area where all houses are required to have steep tile roofs, stucco walls, and small-paned windows to create a European-village look.

The design influences for this house start with the rugged boulder-strewn hillside. The base of the exterior walls uses uncut stones, and the material used in the wall then becomes more refined as the wall rises. The footpaths, which pass between stone walls and pillars, are of sandstone. In contrast to the roughness of the base of the house, the roof is a highly crafted combination of wood and tile. It consists of two layers with an air space between. Air flows from the underside of the overhang, between the roofs, and out a continuous vent near the ridge. This keeps the outer roof cool in the winter, so that snow will remain on the roof and act as insulation.

Between the base and the roof, walls are covered with stucco to give a simple appearance in contrast with other areas.

On the ground floor, entry is through a greenhouse and an inside entry area. From there the living room, the study, and the stairway are just a few steps away. Next to the corner dining room is the kitchen, which includes a large pantry for storing enough food to outlast a blizzard.

Upstairs there are two bedrooms, two baths, a sitting area, an office, and several types of storage closets. A door leads out onto a deck that provides outdoor activity space without altering the natural state of the remaining site.

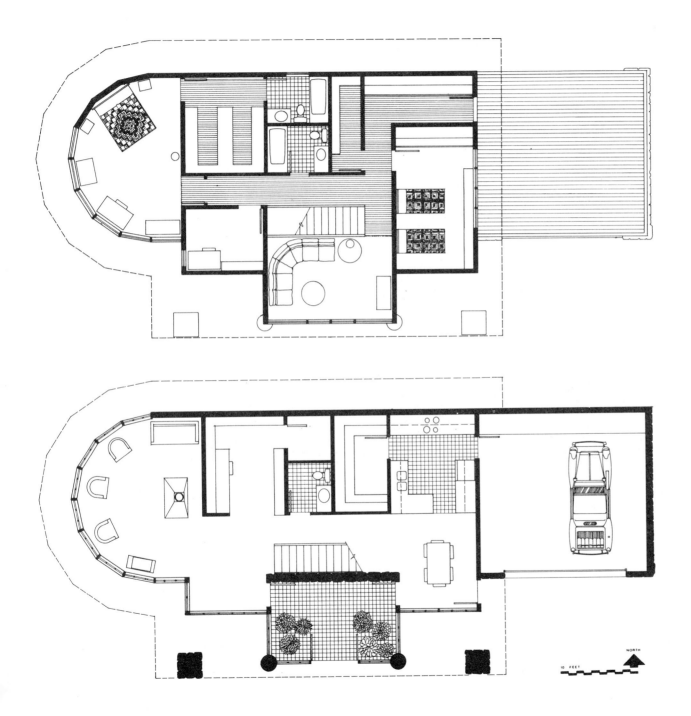

NORTH

10 FEET

Round-Gazebo Home 1950 square feet

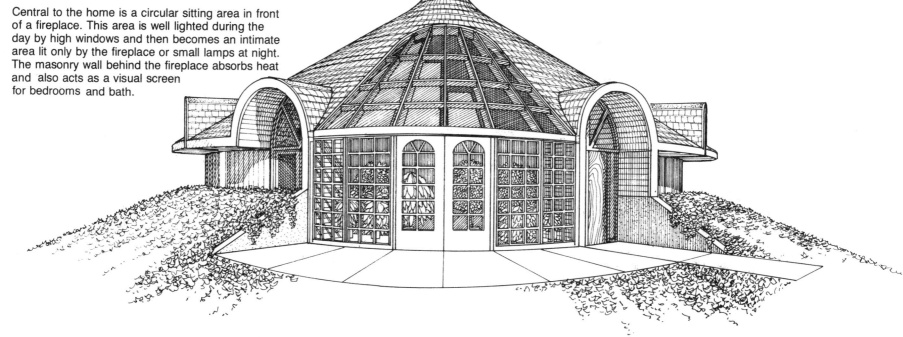

80

This vacation home was designed as a simple retreat for reading, relaxing, and talking—a pavilion away from civilization. It was to have a classical kind of simplicity, possibly evocative of something European, without being imitative. This sunlit house includes a small greenhouse and has views of the outdoors framed through archways.

Central to the home is a circular sitting area in front of a fireplace. This area is well lighted during the day by high windows and then becomes an intimate area lit only by the fireplace or small lamps at night. The masonry wall behind the fireplace absorbs heat and also acts as a visual screen for bedrooms and bath.

The kitchen, utility, and dining rooms are close together for convenience. On the other side of the entry, the study is set off from other areas by furniture.

In homes with round walls it is important to minimize the focusing of sound. This is accomplished by the use of carpeting, padded furniture, and sound-absorbing materials on the walls. These materials, such as fabric-covered sound board, are most effective at the level where sound originates—from two to seven feet above the floor.

Outside, the roof can be covered most easily with cedar shakes because they can be tapered to follow curves. The flattest areas, along the ridges of the curved vaults, are capped with metal to prevent wind from driving water under the shakes.

In developing the site for this design, it is best to let the house stand freely in an open area. Its form is too dramatic to hide between bushes and trees.

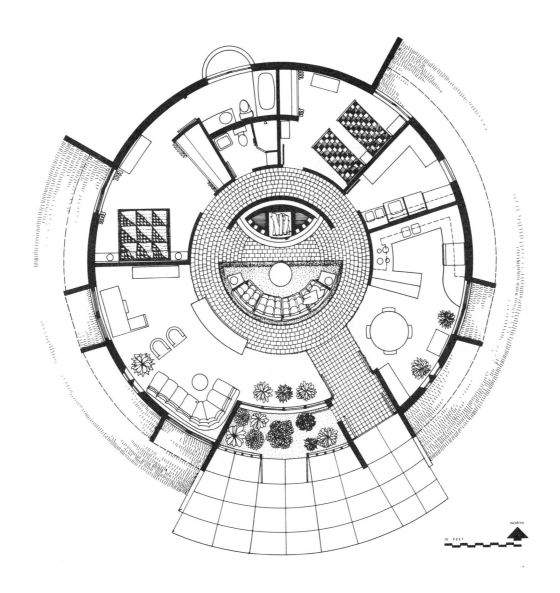

NORTH

10 FEET

Wide A-Frame Home 2050 square feet

The double-pitched roof and cedar siding used for this home are reminiscent of early Northwest Indian homes of the Puget Sound area, and some design elements from that area are incorporated in the round stained-glass windows.

Sometimes site conditions indicate a solution. Here access was from the north, the view was to the south, and there was a moderate slope from west to east combined with frequent strong winds from the west and southwest. The result was an A-frame that was quite wide but not deep. The heavily insulated roof reduces the effect of cooling winds and late-afternoon heat gain, and the projecting walls and corners create turbulence to reduce the speed of the wind. Greenhouse and kitchen windows are very exposed in the morning but fall into shadow by late afternoon.

The main floor steps down the hillside, with the bedrooms highest, then the living room, the dining room, and the kitchen, with the garage at the bottom. Stairs in the living room lead up to a loft that covers the north half of the middle of the house. This could serve as another bedroom, a guest area, or a den. A version of this house was designed for a

couple with grown children who visit occasionally; the three smallest rooms can be used as bedrooms but are most often used as studio and office space. At least one room in a house like this could be equipped with extra electric outlets or a "plug-strip" at table-top height to accommodate a personal computer.

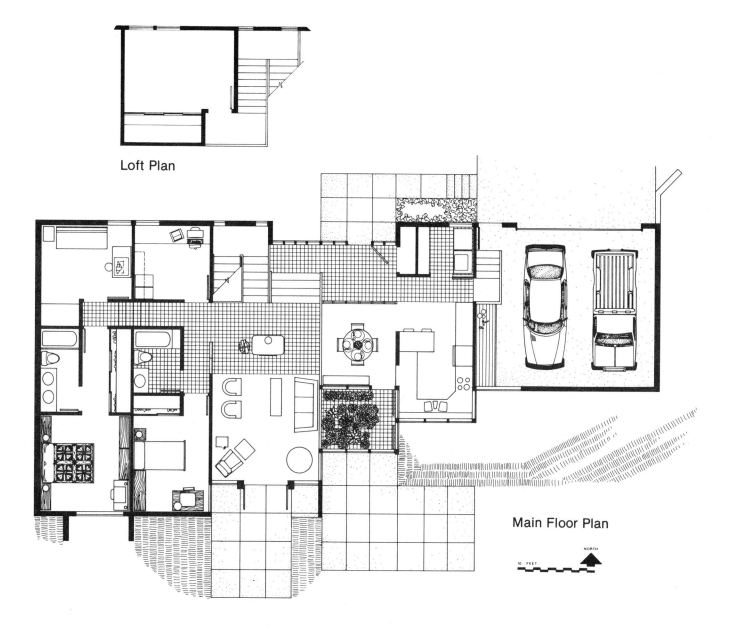

Loft Plan

Main Floor Plan

NORTH

10 FEET

Baroque A-Frame Home 3100 square feet

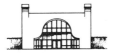

The A-frame became popular years ago for summer
vacation cabins and for use in high-snowfall areas.
Unfortunately, their vaulted ceilings made them difficult to heat, since the ratio of air volume to floor
area was just too high. In this home, however, there
are two floor levels, with protected areas snugly
tucked into berms; a solar greenhouse recessed
into the south side; and social activity areas located
on the upper floor, including a studio workroom and
a recreation room. The ceiling follows the roof line
(see page 110). Hot air originating in the greenhouse moves through the upper floor and is collected near the peak of the ceiling for distribution to
lower areas of the house.

The main floor is composed of a public area—living,
kitchen, dining, and utility rooms—divided from the
bedroom area by the greenhouse and the garage.
Visitors may enter from the greenhouse side or the
garage side, depending on how the house is sited.

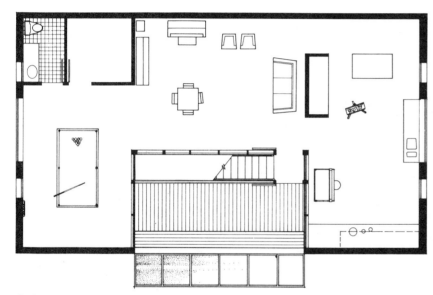

At first this was to be a very angular house with the greenhouse flush with the shake roof, and all plan corners were at right angles. This would be easier to build and to make energy calculations for but produces a less interesting appearance outside and less interesting shadows inside. The curves are somewhat reminiscent of early "shingle style" houses. Often the original concept for a house is so strong that the final version shows no changes in design. It is not unusual, however, to make a series of adjustments and end up with a much different design, as was the case here. This requires constant reevaluation to keep all parts of the design consistent with the overall concept.

10 FEET

NORTH

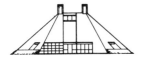

One way to keep snow from sliding off a roof and causing damage is to let the roof go all the way to the ground. Roofs designed for areas of heavy snowfall should offer no obstruction to snow movement or should be designed to hold snow in place. They should also be equal in temperature all the way to the edge, or melting snow will freeze and form icicles and ice dams. Waterproofing must extend as far up the roof as water could be backed up or driven by the wind. Vents and chimneys are least susceptible to damage when placed on the ridge line. On this house, one stack contains the fireplace chimney and the other is an exhaust unit.

Once inside the entry vestibule there is a tiled area for removing wet clothing. The bath is handy to this area for quick changes of clothing. The vestibule is also near the stove for warmth. The large room can be one activity space or it can be divided into three smaller areas by furniture. The north walls, starting at the kitchen, are lined with storage cabinets for seasonal gear, food, and other items.

The other side of the house has two bedrooms, closets, and a storage room that is large enough for a washer and dryer. The large bedroom has both an exterior view and a view into the greenhouse. The smaller bedroom can serve as a den or guest room.

Although this house appears to be all roof, the windows, greenhouse, and high central window would keep the interior quite brightly lit. Areas under the projected roofs are used for storage.

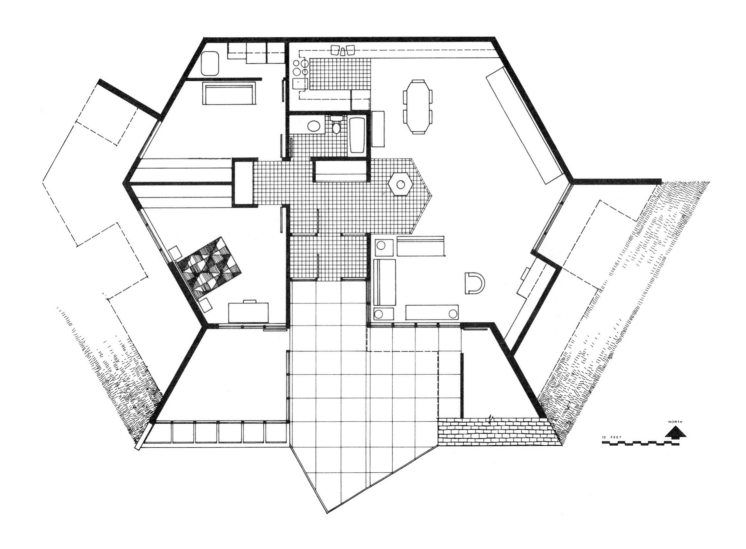

NORTH

10 FEET

Round-Ends Home 1250 square feet

88   The world is full of native dwellings which are basically rectangular in plan but have rounded ends. Some Mayan homes have solid ends for strength but the rest of the home is a webbing of sticks for better ventilation. Some cottages in Europe have rounded thatched roofs instead of high gables. The visual effect is both sheltering and naturalistic, because the rounded corners blend with the rural hills and tree forms.

In this home the bedrooms are widely separated for privacy. They are further secluded by extended wing walls. The master bedroom on the east has a private bath. The other bedroom is also large and has a private sitting area that can accommodate an additional bed.

A wood-burning stove acts as a divider between the living room and the study. Additional warmth is provided by the greenhouse. A skylight along the roof ridge fills the kitchen and dining areas with daylight so there are no dark areas in the house. The north wall is lined with storage cabinets that also add to the effectiveness of the insulation. Since no windows are necessary on this side, the wall outside is mounded with earth up to the roof.

The deck shape repeats the form of the house, as does the shape of the chimney. A hot tub, placed at one end of the deck, has a distant view as well as a close view into the greenhouse. This is a livable and light-filled dwelling that is also energy efficient.

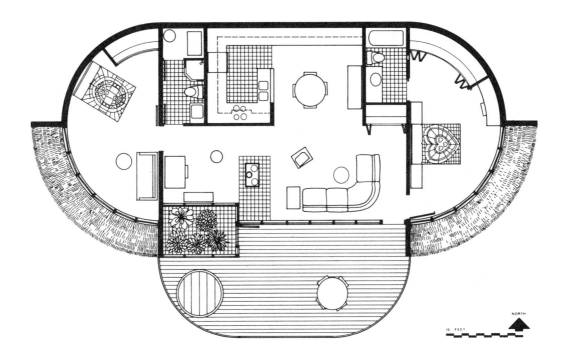

NORTH

10 FEET

Designing Just for Fun

For many people a little innovation isn't enough. Not content with a well-refined solution to the problems of function and environment, they want their house to provide visual interest for every aspect of their

---

The special personalities of some people redefine the meaning of "home." Centuries of theories have attempted to explain unique building designs, but, in many cases, they developed just for fun.

---

lives. The special personalities of some people redefine the meaning of "home." Centuries of theories have attempted to explain unique building designs, but, in many cases, they developed just for fun.

There are people with such unique personalities that they would not fit in any of the previous homes in this book. They would much prefer to live in a tent in the desert or a tree house in the woods than to unpack their belongings in the nicest conventional tract home in all of suburbia. A home with niches labeled bedroom, kitchen, or living room is confining to such people. Their cooking, eating, sleeping, and other activities may not always take place in the same spaces. They see conventional homes and rooms as static and inhibiting, so they long for spaces that can be molded to their lifestyle and still change with their mood and with the seasons.

One approach to designing such homes is to provide a visually neutral open area, protected from weather but otherwise offering as few restrictions as possible. This area becomes a stage for a variety of activities but depends completely on decor for interest. Often such spaces are not inherently interesting because they lack the personality that comes through in articulating functional areas.

Another approach is to design useful spaces that are sculpturally interesting so that each area can be appreciated both for its own visual merit and for the way it is incorporated into daily activities.

The designing of sculptural living spaces requires more than analytic logic. The process is not just the finding of a new way to put a puzzle together and to come up with a new shape. It is the creation of new puzzle pieces, with each shape and space having a new meaning. Windows can be provided in new shapes, locations, and materials, for example, and walls can be covered in new materials or be movable. The home that evolves from this process may cost more to build and will require greater planning and design efforts. Nevertheless, it is an essential investment for a person already too confined by an "ordinary" world.

The key to the success of a unique residential structure is its relevance to the way the occupant actually lives, works, relaxes, and enjoys life. Many bizarre attempts at creativity achieve novelty but not usefulness.

Cultural, environmental, and personal elements combine to generate a personality for a home that illustrates something about the values held by the occupant, but a house also affects the occupant. Many famous houses of historical or political figures are obvious examples. The White House is modified to some degree by each president, and the house, and what it stands for, also modifies the residents. Many people moving into their newly built homes suddenly see their old furniture in a new way. For the first time they realize how much of their self-concept was shaped by their possessions. Architecture is not the only element defining a home: the smell of cooking food, the combination of furnishings and artworks, and the sounds of activities are all parts of the ambience.

Each person experiences each moment of the day in a different way from anyone else. Variation in our lives is part of being human. The final element in home design is the unique personality of the occupant—that collage of personal experiences and relationships. The best designs allow for a wide range of activities both initially and in the future.

Multiple-Circles Home 3100 square feet

Many homes are a collection of small cubicles with specialized uses that have little relation to the rest of the house. In this house, each room is a segment of a larger space, and every area seems to lead to the next. Each room opens up to the outdoors and, at the same time, centers around the fireplace and stair.

As in many earth-sheltered homes, the south side has windows and the north side is mounded with earth. The pantry is built against a mound, and the garage also helps shelter the main house.

The main-floor entry opens to the living room and activity room, the stairs are just ahead, and the kitchen is just around the fireplace. Access from the garage leads to the same central fireplace location. The east entry can function as a mudroom, with a bathroom and laundry handy.

Upstairs, a balcony sitting area overlooks the living room. Adjacent to the loft, a spacious master bedroom suite includes a walk-in closet with a dressing room and a master bath with a large custom bathtub. A second bedroom and bath open onto a large upstairs deck.

Part of the fun of owning a home like this is listening to people try to tell you what it looks like.

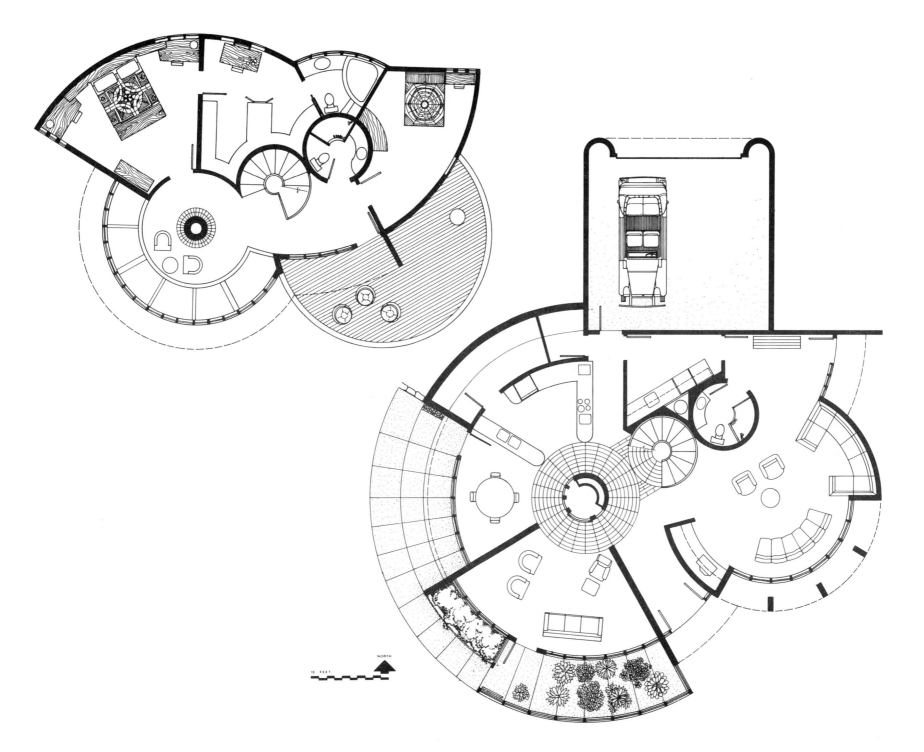

10 FEET

NORTH

Apse Home 2650 square feet

96 If rectangular plans seem too boxy, other forms can be substituted. Many prehistoric structures, including the kivas of the desert Southwest, were round and gave a feeling of protecting the occupants rather than just enclosing them. In much larger buildings, such as cathedrals, rooms projected off the main space had rounded ends. These side apses gave the space a lateral continuity. Curves are also appealing just because they are less common than straight walls. In this home, round shapes are used to denote special areas such as the sunken living room and study, the activity area, and the master bedroom. Other corners are rounded for consistency.

This desert home uses masonry for two reasons: curves are easily formed, and the high mass takes a long time to heat or cool, which helps maintain stable indoor temperatures. Planters also add to the effects of building mass by acting like very thick walls and by reducing reflected heat.

The entry (with a separate garage not shown) includes a guest powder room and can be closed off as a vestibule. From there four choices in direction lead either to the kitchen, the living room, the upstairs, or the craft room. The kitchen, dining area, and activity room are divided only by furniture and location, not by walls. The living room is down two steps to accentuate the feeling of enclosure and to set the area off for conversation. Around the bookcase a smaller apse becomes the study. More shelves divide the study from the craft area.

Upstairs, in addition to three bedrooms and a guest room, a large rooftop patio with a barbecue is a major activity area with views that can't be seen from the yard.

A good way to shade windows in the apses would be with shades on rollers that are pulled from the bottom up. The length of shaded area would be different on each window, and the pattern of shades raised to differing heights could be quite interesting.

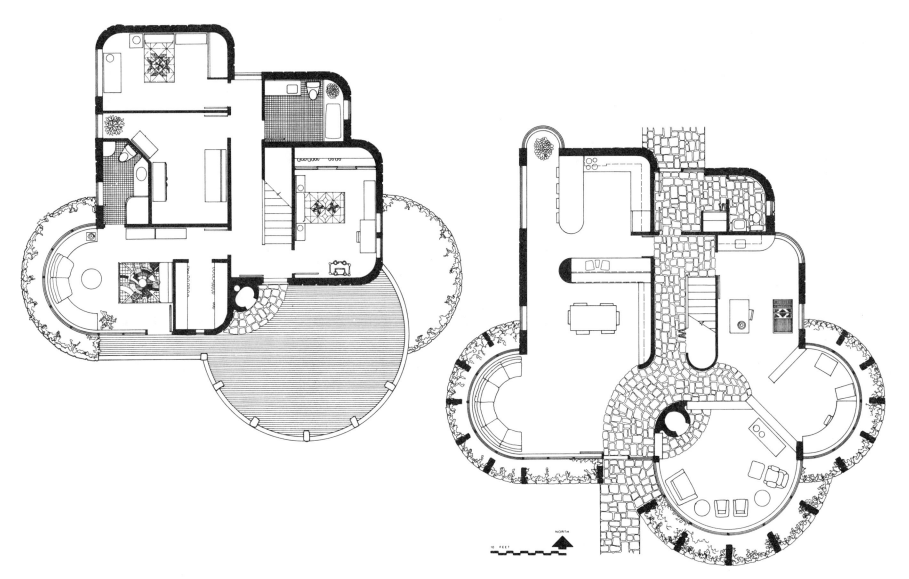

NORTH

10 FEET

Curved-Wall Home 2000 square feet

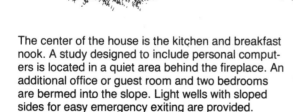

Often in a very rugged natural setting the standard shape of a rectilinear box doesn't seem appropriate. This design is for a home nestled into a rock out-cropping atop a cliff. It is reached by a trail from the garage. The living, dining, and activity areas form one long room with rounded ends that take advantage of the 180-degree view. Beams radiate from two wood columns to the outside walls.

Due to the steep site, the greenhouse is down a level from the house and is reached by a walkway and an exterior door. It is on the southeast side of the house so it will warm up early in the morning and overheating will be minimized in the afternoon. Warm air rises directly from the greenhouse through vents below the windows into the main house.

The center of the house is the kitchen and breakfast nook. A study designed to include personal comput-ers is located in a quiet area behind the fireplace. An additional office or guest room and two bedrooms are bermed into the slope. Light wells with sloped sides for easy emergency exiting are provided.

Rounding a roof immediately limits the materials that can be economically used. Cedar shakes are the easiest to apply, but some tiles will also follow a curve.

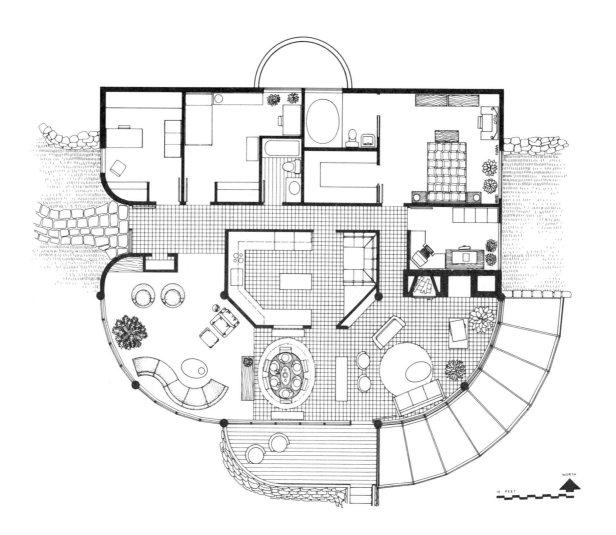

NORTH

10 FEET

Curved-Partition Home 1400 square feet

100   For the sake of economy, the structure for this home is a simple square that consists of two retaining walls on the north sides and wood posts that support a truss joist roof. Interior walls and dividers are nonbearing, so they can curve to give a free-flowing quality to the space. The wall between the front room and the office, for example, is only five feet high so that it provides some privacy without boxing in either room. At the entry, a screen wall hides the dining area from anyone coming to the door.

The kitchen provides for the minimal needs of a person who cooks for himself only occasionally. For most people, the sink, stove, and refrigerator would be spread over a larger area to provide convenient counter space.

The north corner of the bedroom is a light-well garden that provides a private view and an emergency fire escape.

Although the supports for the deck are straight, the ends of the decking are cut in a large curve to complement the curve of the front window.

The curved wall of the bathroom provides a private outside view, and, from the outside, a way to separate the mass of the house visually from the hillside.

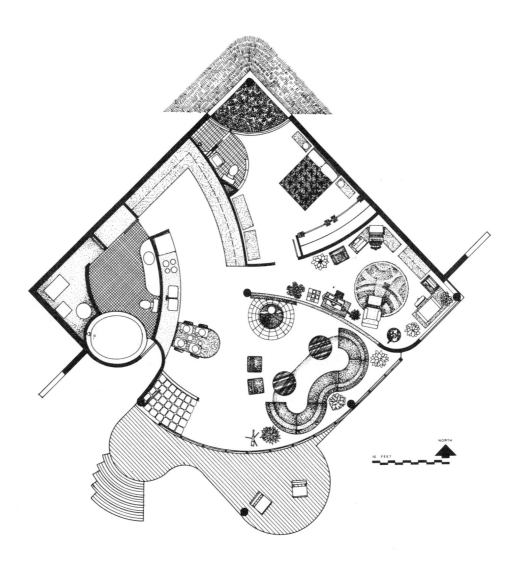

NORTH

10 FEET

Pyramid Home 2000 square feet

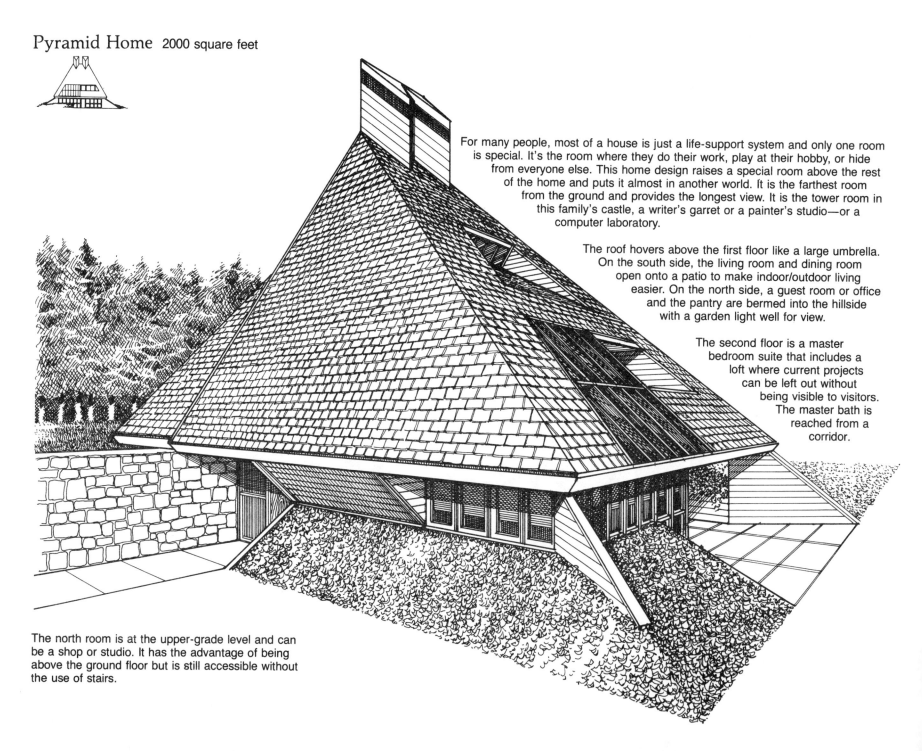

For many people, most of a house is just a life-support system and only one room is special. It's the room where they do their work, play at their hobby, or hide from everyone else. This home design raises a special room above the rest of the home and puts it almost in another world. It is the farthest room from the ground and provides the longest view. It is the tower room in this family's castle, a writer's garret or a painter's studio—or a computer laboratory.

The roof hovers above the first floor like a large umbrella. On the south side, the living room and dining room open onto a patio to make indoor/outdoor living easier. On the north side, a guest room or office and the pantry are bermed into the hillside with a garden light well for view.

The second floor is a master bedroom suite that includes a loft where current projects can be left out without being visible to visitors. The master bath is reached from a corridor.

The north room is at the upper-grade level and can be a shop or studio. It has the advantage of being above the ground floor but is still accessible without the use of stairs.

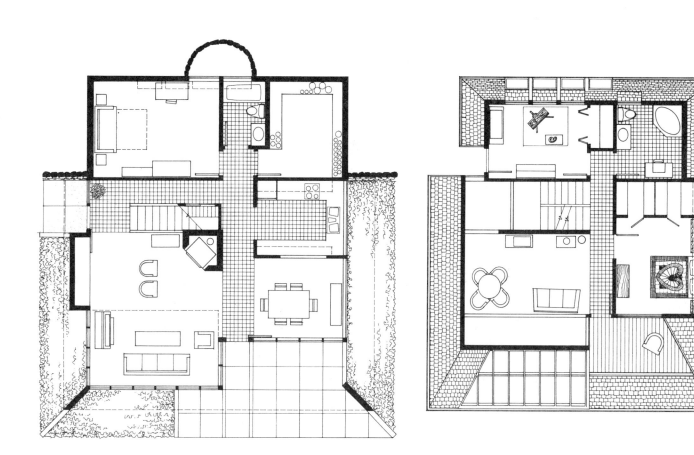

NORTH

10 FEET

Central-Lantern Home 3400 square feet

This compact house resulted from a study of a lot my parents were once thinking of buying. Often a good way to evaluate the purchase of property is to go through the first stages of design and see if your desires for the land can really be fulfilled. In this case, a lot of setback requirements decreased the buildable area to the point where the property was not usable and the project was shelved.

A square plan was selected for economy, but it was turned forty-five degrees on the lot so that two sides would have a view. Since the lot was not aligned on a north-south grid, this angle was also necessary in order to face a wall to the south. The living room opens to the corner balcony to reduce feelings of confinement. The corner greenhouse in this light-frame home has eutectic salt containers between studs in the wall that divides the greenhouse from the bedroom. These containers can store a large amount of heat and release it slowly as the house starts to cool. Eutectic salts provide the thermal time lag advantages of high mass without the weight.

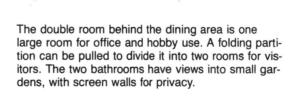

The double room behind the dining area is one large room for office and hobby use. A folding partition can be pulled to divide it into two rooms for visitors. The two bathrooms have views into small gardens, with screen walls for privacy.

Although this plan includes an optional unfinished basement, it could also be built as just one story with the loft. The roof is flush with the walls on the north sides and overhangs on the south. High windows admit light and views to the loft area. Heat is collected at the peak of this space and ducted to the basement fan unit for recirculation.

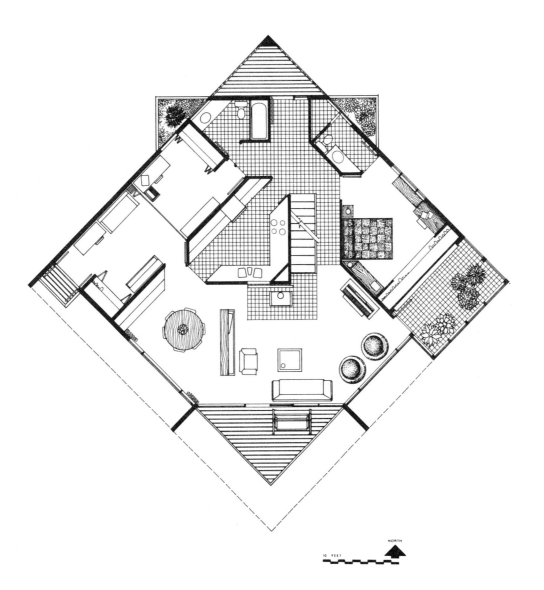

NORTH

10 FEET

Barrel-Vault Home   1600 square feet

Construction systems are now widely available from reputable distributors for concrete structures that require no formwork. Flat or precurved metal plates, which will remain in place in the final structure as reinforcing, are connected and then sprayed with concrete. In an arch form, these structures are very strong even though they are not very thick. Many shapes are possible, but they all require engineering analysis.

This home is a two-story vaulted structure with a one-story vaulted living room and an entry that extends to include a greenhouse pavilion or sun room. A dome skylight atop the largest vault lets sunlight into the upper story and on down through an opening to the lowest floor. A cover on the skylight can be rotated to provide shade in the summer or reflect additional light and heat into the home in the winter. A smaller cap on the greenhouse is an exhaust fan.

The living room includes a wood-burning stove, and heat from that area rises up to the rest of the house. Up a few steps, the kitchen is extended to provide a utility area. Steps lead up to the loft and down to a wine cellar/pantry. The master suite includes a bath with a tub that projects out into the backyard. This would need modification in less private neighborhoods. The adjacent room can be used as a study and guest room. Upstairs is a seating alcove, a bedroom, a bath, and an extra room for crafts or other use.

As with the curved-wall homes, materials must be used to absorb sound and prevent focusing or traveling of sound along a curved surface.

(For building section, see page 110.)

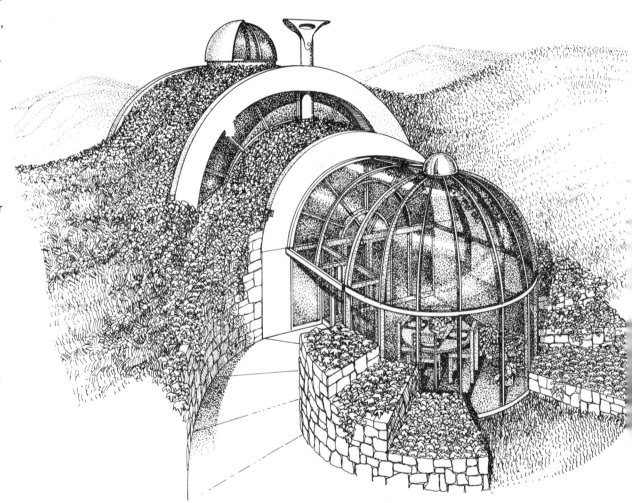

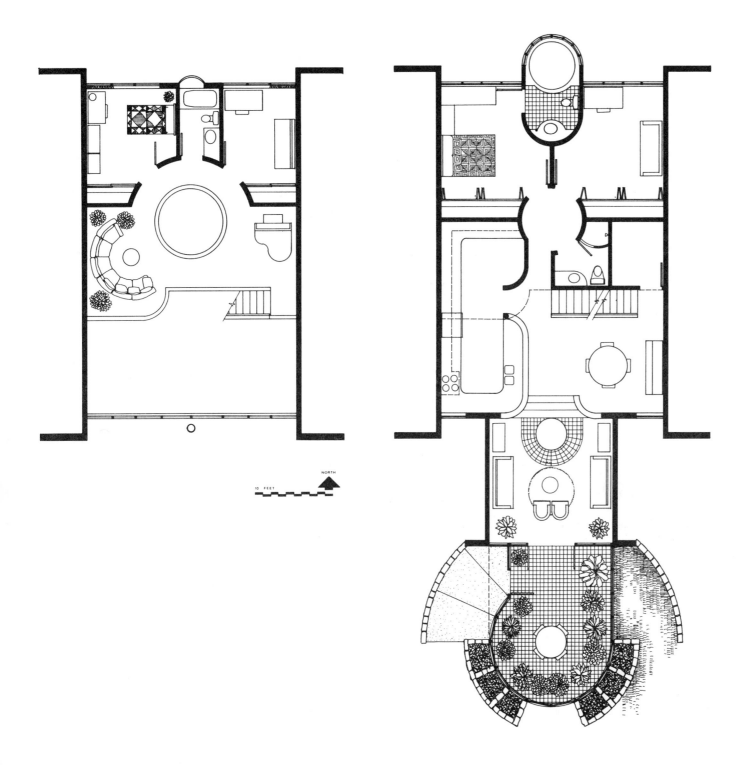

NORTH

10 FEET

Free-Form Home   2450 square feet

Houses don't really need to have straight walls. With materials such as brick, block, or stone, curved walls are actually stronger than straight ones. Curves can also be formed with boards, beams, or trusses by placing each one at a slightly different angle than the last one. Twisted shapes called hyperbolic paraboloids are made this way. Other materials, including plywood, can be bent before or during construction so curves can be created in many ways. For complicated shapes it is often easier to mold a shape or spray a material onto a reinforcing framework. Temporary shapes can also be used as frames. Domes, for example, have been created over giant balloons. Highly complex shapes are now being made using chopped fiberglass as reinforcing for sprayed concrete. The shape of this home was developed to give the feeling that it could have grown right on the site. Many combinations of structural systems could be used to create the forms, depending on the budget and available construction expertise.

Although the rooms have very unusual shapes, their interrelationship is similar to many other homes in this book. The living room, kitchen, and family room are all located on the south side for maximum daylight. Behind those rooms are two bedrooms that project out enough to capture some southern sun. The back of the house is a garage and an office.

Upstairs there are two bedrooms, a bath, and a loft space. The loft looks down into the living room and family room and on out through arched openings to the outdoors.

NORTH

10 FEET

110 On this page sections are shown cut in a
north/south axis through six of the homes. If you
picture the sun on the right, you can imagine the
variety of ways sunlight and heat are admitted into
each house. At high window areas light is allowed
to reach well into the home.

Although each of these homes was developed for a
specific geographic location, modifications to the
window area and exterior materials could widely
extend the range of suitability of any of the plans.
Analysis is required not only for the specific site, but
also for the way in which the owner is willing to
operate the home. A home and its energy-modifying
devices can be operated manually or by computer,
or the house can be so sheltered that no operation
of any device is required if the occupant can toler-
ate moderate air-temperature fluctuations.

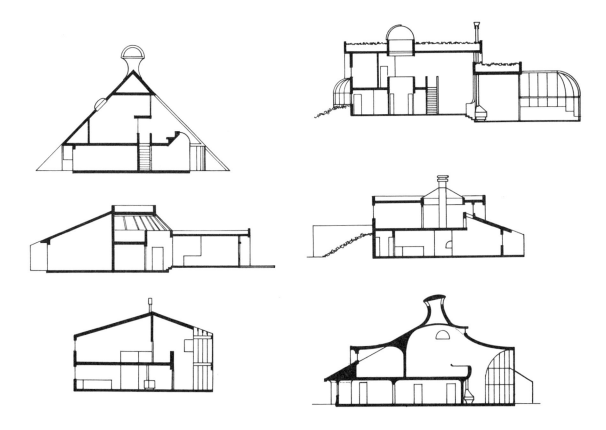

Index

About This Book

When designing a custom home, if we reflect on the client's past history, present understanding, and future aspirations, it would seem very strange to develop an ordinary house. The thirty-two homes in this book are intended to broaden the range of homes that could be built in normal settings and, with a few exceptions, on a budget similar to other custom homes. It is hoped that one of them will provide a starting point in the design of your next home. The first few homes are based on variations of homes designed by Jeremy Jones for his own architectural firm and for a partnership in Spokane, Washington. None of the homes were built exactly the way they are shown in the book. They have been changed in the book either to extend the variety of examples or to protect the uniqueness of the home for the owner. It seemed best to not have anyone duplicate a home that already existed. Earlier homes are illustrated in *Homes in the Earth*, a book coauthored by Jones.

Jeremy Jones graduated from the University of Washington in 1968 and has worked in Washington, Arizona, and Colorado on a wide range of projects in twelve states. Currently he is a designer and illustrator for the Denver architectural firm of Rogers Nagel Langhart.

Early editions of the text were sent to Pamela Simon of Tucson, Arizona, for editing, suggestions, and amplification. Simon is a University of Washington graduate in home economics and has taught at the secondary level in Washington and Arizona. She is also a textile artist specializing in quilts.

Sketches and text were turned over to Susan Ficca for book design, layout, and cover design. Ficca, who has a BFA from Colorado State University, is a graphic artist in Denver who has produced designs for a wide range of items, from corporate logos to the painting of a helicopter.

Today the design of almost any building is a complex process. We now use computers to analyze needs, determine costs, suggest room arrangements, and even do some drawing. But the design process goes beyond the strictly rational methods that can be computer aided. The design of a home requires an understanding of personality, tradition, and many things even less tangible. Until the computer can feel the grass between its toes, fall in love against reason, see the familiar moon rise over a foreign sea, or try to make a child eat cooked carrots, designing a home for creative living will remain an art.